Shortcuts
to Inner Peace

70 SIMPLE PATHS TO EVERYDAY SERENITY

ASHLEY DAVIS BUSH, L.C.S.W.

BERKLEY BOOKS, NEW YORK

THE BERKLEY PUBLISHING GROUP
Published by the Penguin Group
Penguin Group (USA) Inc.
375 Hudson Street, New York, New York 10014, USA

Penguin Group (Canada), 90 Eglinton Avenue East, Suite 700, Toronto, Ontario M4P 2Y3, Canada
(a division of Pearson Penguin Canada Inc.)
Penguin Books Ltd., 80 Strand, London WC2R 0RL, England
Penguin Group Ireland, 25 St. Stephen's Green, Dublin 2, Ireland (a division of Penguin Books Ltd.)
Penguin Group (Australia), 250 Camberwell Road, Camberwell, Victoria 3124, Australia
(a division of Pearson Australia Group Pty. Ltd.)
Penguin Books India Pvt. Ltd., 11 Community Centre, Panchsheel Park, New Delhi—110 017, India
Penguin Group (NZ), 67 Apollo Drive, Rosedale, Auckland 0632, New Zealand
(a division of Pearson New Zealand Ltd.)
Penguin Books (South Africa) (Pty.) Ltd., 24 Sturdee Avenue, Rosebank, Johannesburg 2196,
South Africa

Penguin Books Ltd., Registered Offices: 80 Strand, London WC2R 0RL, England

This book is an original publication of The Berkley Publishing Group.

Copyright © 2011 by Ashley Davis Bush.
Cover art: Olive branch copyright © by Lauren Burke / Getty Images.
Cover design by Diana Kolsky.
Interior text design by Laura K. Corless.

PRINTING HISTORY
Berkley trade paperback edition / November 2011

Library of Congress Cataloging-in-Publication Data

Bush, Ashley Davis.
  Shortcuts to inner peace : 70 simple paths to everyday serenity / Ashley Davis Bush.
    p. cm.
  Includes bibliographical references.
  ISBN 978-0-425-24324-4 (pbk.)
 1. Relaxation. 2. Peace of mind. I. Title.
  RA785.B878   2011
  613.7'92—dc23   2011023461

PRINTED IN THE UNITED STATES OF AMERICA

10 9 8 7 6 5 4 3 2 1

PUBLISHER'S NOTE: Neither the publisher nor the author is engaged in rendering professional advice
or services to the individual reader. The ideas, procedures, and suggestions contained in this book are
not intended as a substitute for consulting with your physician. All matters regarding your health
require medical supervision. Neither the author nor the publisher shall be liable or responsible for any
loss or damage allegedly arising from any information or suggestion in this book.

Praise for
Shortcuts to Inner Peace

"*Shortcuts to Inner Peace* mines mindfulness techniques in a [c]... ful, easy-to-apply way. Following the exercises would chang... ... one's day for the better."

> —Sharon Salzberg, author of *Real Happiness and Lovingkindness*

"The peace we seek is right inside us. Ashley Davis Bush's 'Shortcuts' are simple yet powerful techniques that train the mind and heart to more naturally access this inner peace."

> —James Baraz, coauthor of *Awakening Joy*, founder of
> Spirit Rock Meditation Center

"Ashley Davis Bush helps you take doable steps that are truly shortcuts to happiness and inner strength. I love this down-to-earth, honest, and useful book."

> —Rick Hanson, Ph.D., coauthor of *Buddha's Brain*

"If your life is too busy to meditate, this book is for you. It's a treasure trove of elegant strategies for freeing the mind from its own devices."

> —Christopher K. Germer, Ph.D., coauthor of
> *The Mindful Path to Self-Compassion*

"I'd recommend this to anyone who wants to live a richer, more peaceful life."

> —Elisha Goldstein, Ph.D., coauthor of *A Mindfulness-Based
> Stress Reduction Workbook*

"*Shortcuts to Inner Peace* will bring forth an immediate breath of fresh air. Read this wonderful and creative book now and set the compass of your life on a new direction."

> —Ronald A. Alexander, Ph.D., coauthor of *Wise Mind Open Mind*

"Practicing just one of these Shortcuts could well transform your life. This b[ook]...

> ...[t] Meditation:
> ...ple on the Go

"Ashley Davis Bush is a virtuoso at creatively sneaking mindfulness into daily activities." —Bodhipaksa, author of *Living As a River*

"We highly recommend this book to inspire a calmer and more peaceful life."
—C. Alexander Simpkins, Ph.D., and Annellen M. Simpkins, Ph.D., authors of *Zen Meditation in Psychotherapy*

"*Shortcuts to Inner Peace* should be required reading for anyone living in the twenty-first century."
—Shawn M. Talbott, Ph.D., author of *The Secret of Vigor*

"Ashley Davis Bush's *Shortcuts to Inner Peace* is a treasure chest of simple and effective ways to quiet your mind and body."
—Fred Gallo, Ph.D., Energy Psychology pioneer and coauthor of *Energy Tapping for Trauma*

"Ashley Davis Bush offers an imaginative array of tools, redirecting readers' awareness toward mindful, peaceful responses to everyday stress triggers."
—Susie Mantell, author of *Your Present: A Half-Hour of Peace*

"These 'Shortcuts' are powerful tools for reconnecting with calm, finding balance, and choosing joy."
—Michelle May, M.D., author of *Eat What You Love, Love What You Eat*

"*Shortcuts* is practical and transformative."
—Allan Lokos, author of *Pocket Peace*

"Easy to read, easy to do; you won't be disappointed."
—Dawn Huebner, Ph.D., coauthor of *What to Do When You Worry Too Much*

For my soul mate, Daniel,
whose "lake of calm" beckoned me

Acknowledgments

It is a thrill beyond words to have written this book. I was fortunate to have had many helpful cooks in the kitchen, and I'm grateful to each of them for their role in bringing this recipe to life.

My literary agent, John Willig, was like a beacon of light with his immediate enthusiastic support of this project. Every interaction with John, from my first e-mail to my most recent conversation, has been a delight. He brings his optimism and insightful guidance to every encounter. I feel especially fortunate to have John on my side.

Reuniting with my editor, Denise Silvestro, has been a tremendous blessing. She brought *Transcending Loss* to life over fifteen years ago, and likewise, she shepherded this book with her customary care, keen eye, and thoughtful touch. I will always be grateful to Denise for how she helped to shape and encourage my voice in the world.

I extend a heartfelt thanks to all the folks at Berkley Books, those I've met and those I haven't—from the mail-room intern to the president, from the copyeditor to the cover designer—all of us working together to make this book a reality.

Over the years, there were many guides whose writings, workshops, and websites added to my personal "compost" of ideas. Many of these people will never know how much they influenced me, but I send them my gratitude. Also, I am grateful to my clients for their fearless desire to grow and their willingness to share their journeys with me. My work is both a sacred calling and a profound privilege.

I am especially appreciative of both Women Supporting Women in Exeter, New Hampshire, and also to Exeter Health Resources for being early supporters of my Shortcuts and offering me a forum for developing my materials.

To the readers of the manuscript, I offer special thanks for their insightful feedback: Elliott Baker, Judith Bush, Glenn Corey, Peyton Lewis, Nagabodi, Saddhamala, Nancy Shappell, and Nancy Webb.

Aryaloka Buddhist Center, a place of deep serenity and peacefulness, offered me a place of true respite and repose. There I have been and continue to be supported and guided on my journey to access inner peace. Likewise, Star Island and Emery House have been spiritual homes for over a decade, repeatedly bringing me back to my essence.

My dear soul sister, Martha Nossiff, is ever in my heart as a fellow pilgrim striving to live from a place of peace. She has been with me through every high and every low over the past fourteen years. Her devotion and blessed friendship know no bounds.

I am indebted to my dear parents, Peyton Lewis and William Davis, for giving me the gift of life.

And to my children and stepchildren—Elizabeth, Channing, Victoria, Setse, and Inle—I express gratitude for their love and their amazing presence in my life. They are tremendous teachers for me on my path of inner peace.

To my husband, Daniel, there are no words to adequately convey my gratitude. Without him, this book simply would not exist. Not only has he been my first reader, my patient editor, and overall champion, he has also been my teacher, student, guide, and companion on the path. His transformative love has opened me to a whole new level of living.

Finally, with humility, I express my deepest gratitude to my Muse, the great Universal Spirit that blows through me. I continue to be amazed at the music that comes forth, knowing that I am but the instrument. May this melody inspire you as much as it has inspired me.

Contents

Prologue   *1*

Stress Alert   *5*

Shortcut Solutions   *17*

The Thread Basics

YOUR DAILY THREAD
Shortcuts to Weave Through Your Day   *33*

> *Daily Dose*   *35*
> *Morning Glories*   *37*
> *Catch and Release*   *39*
> *Freeze Frame*   *41*
> *Stop, Drop, and Roll*   *43*
> *Go with the Flow*   *46*
> *Take Five*   *49*
> *Big Sky*   *51*
> *Shakedown*   *53*
> *Rest in Peace*   *55*

SHALL WE DANCE?
Shortcuts to Weave Through Your Relationships   *57*

> *Mirror, Mirror on the Wall*   *61*
> *My Sunshine*   *63*

Love Letters   **66**

Rise and Fall   **69**

Jack 'n' Chill   **72**

Right Turn   **75**

Win-Win   **78**

Rag Doll   **81**

Smooth Scaling   **84**

Cheesecloth   **87**

SENSORY SPOTLIGHT

Shortcuts to Weave Mindfully   **91**

Touch Tank   **94**

Lend a Hand   **97**

Almond Joy   **100**

See-Food   **102**

Crystal Flame   **105**

Double Take   **107**

Stop 'n' Smell   **109**

Hair-Raising   **111**

Ring My Bell   **114**

A Little Night Music   **116**

The Peace Portals

CHILL OUT!

Shortcuts to Calm Your Body   **121**

How Low Can You Go?   **124**

Dish It Out   **126**

Play It Again, Sam   **128**

Under the Sea   **130**

Tap Dance   **132**

Be a Tree **134**

Take the Pulse **136**

Eyewitness **139**

Fancy Feet **141**

Dial It Down **143**

THINK AGAIN

Shortcuts to Quiet Your Mind **145**

Time Travel **149**

Take Dictation **151**

Remember This **153**

Glad Game **155**

Take Me Away **157**

Watch Your Mouth **159**

You Can Say That *Again* **162**

Magic Glasses **164**

Half 'n' Half **166**

Outstanding **169**

ALL YOU NEED IS LOVE

Shortcuts to Open Your Heart **171**

God Bless Us, Every One **176**

Don't Bug Me **178**

Who Is Your Mother? **180**

Newspaper Clippings **182**

At Your Service **185**

Pretty Baby **188**

Rags to Riches **191**

Some Pig **194**

Blooming **196**

Open Sesame **198**

WAKE UP, LITTLE HONEY, WAKE UP!
Shortcuts to Connect with Spirit   **201**

      Amazing Grace   **206**

      Myku   **209**

      Hot Air   **212**

      Fair-Weather Friend   **214**

      White Flag   **217**

      Finger Food   **219**

      Bless You   **222**

      Tuned In   **224**

      Let Your Fingers Do the Walking   **226**

      Joy to the World   **229**

Deep Peace   **231**

Appendices

      Shortcut "Tools and Triggers" Cross-Referencing   **237**

      Shortcut Contemplation: "ABC" Connection   **248**

      Shortcut Contemplation: Peace Connection   **250**

Suggested Reading   **251**

Deep peace of the running wave to you
Deep peace of the flowing air to you
Deep peace of the quiet earth to you
Deep peace of the shining stars to you
Deep peace of the gentle night to you
Moon and stars pour their healing light on you

—GAELIC BLESSING

Prologue

The alarm clock breaks her slumber. *Beep . . . beep . . . beep.* Before getting out of bed, Susan's mind starts racing: *Big presentation at work today!* She walks to the bathroom, brushes her teeth, showers, and gets dressed—all on autopilot. Her mind is preoccupied and agitated. Suddenly realizing that she has lost track of time, she begins to rush. In her hurry to get out the door, she spills coffee all over her khaki pants.

"Oh, $%#@!!!!" she yells. Her shoulders tense and she throws the cup in the sink. "Damn it! I'm such a *klutz*." She stomps upstairs to change, cursing the fact that she's ruined her pants and barely can afford to have them dry-cleaned. *My life is a disaster*, she thinks.

With her heart beating wildly and knowing that she'll now be late for work, she rushes to her car and tears out of her driveway. She speeds recklessly, cutting people off in traffic and creating a ripple of negative energy in everyone she passes. And then . . . the sound of a siren. Susan is overwhelmed with frustration and rage.

Her negative thoughts spin out: *I have the worst luck in the world. I don't deserve this ticket. My boss is going to be furious with me for being this late. I'll probably blow the presentation and . . . what if I get fired? My day is trashed.*

When Susan gets to work, her stomach is tied in knots and her back stiff. She enters the office like a dark cloud and performs badly during the presentation. That night, Susan goes home feeling like a failure.

Poor Susan. She blames the spilled coffee for triggering the chain of events that started her terrible day. Like most of us, she points to an unhappy event as the cause of her troubles—not realizing that it was *how* she reacted to the situation, not the situation itself, that ruined her day.

We are rarely aware of how our thoughts trigger our reactions to stress. The time between an event and our response to the event is so short that we don't even notice the negative thought in the background. When we are not aware of our background thinking, this is what it looks like: coffee spills . . . (*Damn*) . . . "Oh, $%#@!!!!" In the nanosecond that follows the spilled coffee comes the thought and stressful feeling (*Damn*), followed immediately and unconsciously by profanity. On the other hand, when we *are* consciously aware of our background thinking, there is a pause after the stressful thought and we notice a "fork in the road." A choice becomes available to us:

We can follow our usual road, swearing and getting upset, or we can observe and shift, thereby choosing an entirely new trajectory.

So, can we train ourselves to pause? Can we learn to actually derail the habituated response and proceed intentionally? Can we develop new reactions to stress, new habits that not only lessen our suffering but actually increase our inner peace?

Yes! Practicing Shortcuts, that is, well-being exercises that are linked to established daily patterns, makes our lives more peaceful. Shortcuts (tools linked to triggers) allow us to experience calmness and clarity, acceptance and gratitude, love and connection on a regular basis. They help us develop new habits of pausing, habits of redirection away from stress, and habits of "waking up" to life's riches. Moreover, when we're in a potentially downward stress spiral (and it happens to all of us), we can use Shortcuts to react differently . . . to respond peacefully.

Imagine that Susan had been practicing the Shortcuts as daily habits for a few months before her big presentation. Let's watch her day unfold as tools become triggered by her activities and experiences:

The alarm clock breaks her slumber. *Beep . . . beep . . . beep.* Before getting out of bed, Susan's mind starts setting her peaceful intention ("Daily Dose"). Brushing her teeth, she opens herself with curiosity to the day's activities ("Morning Glories"). As she showers, she lets her worries go down the drain ("Catch and Release"), and then she gets dressed. Suddenly realizing that she has lost track of time, she begins to rush. In her hurry to get out the door, she spills her coffee all over her khaki pants.

She gasps . . . (*Damn*) . . . and shakes her head, aware that she is at a fork in the road; she makes a choice. She takes a slow deep breath to center and redirect herself ("How Low Can You Go?"). As Susan changes her pants, she laughs and shifts her attention to things in her life for which she's grateful ("Glad Game").

On the road to work, she opens her heart to others ("Stop, Drop, and Roll"). Before her presentation, she relaxes with a visualization that helps shift her energy ("Take Me Away"). Susan continues through her day feeling confident and calm.

Impossible? Not really. Shortcuts that are triggered throughout our day help us to access the well of inner peace that *already exists* within us. If we do lose our cool, using these tools will interrupt the spin cycle of stressful thoughts so we can get back on track. Over time, as we intentionally redirect our responses to stress, the neural pathways in our brains actually change, "wiring" us for new, more peaceful responses to life.

Which reaction to spilled coffee would you rather have?

Stress Alert

I was forty-four years old when, at my initiation, my first husband and I separated. Having slowly but surely grown apart over the years, and after months (if not years) of talks and tears and intense soul searching, I had finally gotten to the point where the pain of holding on to the marriage was more painful than letting it go.

During the year in which we were negotiating our divorce (which, I'm happy to say, was an amicable process), we made arrangements for our three children to stay in the "marital" house while we took turns coming and going. In the divorce industry, this temporary solution is known as "nesting." I went between the house and a small nearby apartment, and my first husband went between the house and a corporate apartment on the West Coast.

So there I was, in transition, full of hope and fear, sadness and possibility. I look back on that year as being one of super stress: the sadness of a life ending, my children's painful reactions, extended family and friends' anguished responses, financial strains. There were many nights in my new part-time apartment when I cried my eyes out, not sure how I would get through the next day. It was an awkward, in-between life chapter like nothing I had ever experienced.

In the spirit of reducing the stress in my life, I searched out some new activities. I joined a regular yoga class and I learned meditation through a local Buddhist center. The contemplative techniques I learned were interesting, extremely helpful . . . and extremely time consuming. Over the months, I dropped out of the classes because I was "too busy." Each jewel of a tool seemed to join the pile of the "I know I shoulds . . . but I don't have the time." I had a growing collection of good intentions— brought out at New Year's and then back in the closet by Valentine's Day.

Fast-forward several years . . . I'm living in a blended family of my new husband, five children (four of whom are teenagers), and five pets. Because of the various joint-custody patterns that my husband and I have, there is a different constellation of children in the house every few days. Talk about stress!

Even without the emotional upheavals, just having so many moving parts in one household was enough to make this ever-so-slightly tidy woman—okay, I'll admit it, uptight obsessive compulsive—go crazy. For a long time, I found that when we had two, three, or all five kids at home, I just about came unglued. The influx of energy—stuff, noise, music, demands, needs, tensions, groceries, laundry, homework—completely flooded me.

I knew that exercise and meditation would be helpful, but I just couldn't make the time. Between work, writing, managing a household, focusing on my marriage, and dealing with the children and animals, I felt like I was lucky to eat and sleep.

Stressed Out

Let's face it, sometimes life can feel relentless. Most of us feel like we're on some version of a gerbil wheel trying to balance work, relationships, home, health, and leisure time (with leisure time usually coming in last place). And just when you have one area worked out to your satisfaction, something goes out of whack in another area. It's as if we never get caught up—the trash is emptied and another basket is filled, the bills are paid and the next round comes in, the e-mails are answered and a dozen more pop up.

There's *always* something to do, someone to get back to, something to pay, somewhere to go, and something to clean, fix, adjust, improve, or organize on the endless wheel of life. Circumstances are constantly in flux so that in spite of our diligence, life presents us with one task after another.

On top of the strains of ordinary daily living, we have giant sources of stress in life-changing events: death, divorce, unemployment, a move, major illness, bankruptcy, foreclosure, war. Honestly, life can sometimes feel like climbing a mountain— uphill all the way.

In the twenty-first century, we're not just supersizing our French fries and sodas, we're supersizing our stress levels. And it's not just the external tensions in life that mount up. There are a whole range of "inner world" stresses that wreak havoc with our psyches: fear, anxiety, worry, depression, low self-esteem, perfectionism, commitment phobia, expectations, inadequacy, self-imposed pressures, self-loathing, resentments, secrets, lies, judgments, terror of death, among dozens of others. I feel my blood pressure rising just listing these.

Speaking of rising blood pressure, stress really takes a toll on our bodies. Living in a perpetual fight-or-flight state creates some very unwelcome chronic levels of chemicals in our systems, principally adrenaline and cortisol. This may be why stress-related disorders—hypertension, panic attacks, ulcers, gastrointestinal disorders, adrenal fatigue, immune deficiencies, heart disease, chronic fatigue, to name a few—drive us in droves to the doctor. A recent study by the American Psychological Association stated that 75 percent of adults reported moderate to high levels of stress in the prior month (that's upward of 230 million stressed people!). One half of those reported that their stress had increased in the previous year.

What Is Stress?

Stress is our reaction to stimuli, both real and imagined. This rapid response is characterized by increased energy, increased heart rate and hyperarousal. When stress is excessive and continuous, most of us experience the discomfort of the strain, the pressure, and the feeling of being overwhelmed that we all know so well. Interestingly, these negative physical and mental reactions are not relegated only to harsh times in our lives. Stress also occurs with positive life events—like getting married, having a baby, getting a coveted new job, or retiring. It is often surprising how the impact of stress can contaminate even celebratory life events.

Stress in excess causes an unhealthy "high alert!" response that eventually wears down the body. And furthermore, many of our "coping" mechanisms actually create even *more* stress in our lives. Drinking to excess, overeating, gambling, overspending, compulsive computer use, or television watching can all cause more problems than the original stressors. While these "solutions" may feel like a relief in the moment, they instead create anesthetized lives.

Ironically, we feed our stress by blaming our circumstances for our condition rather than seeing how we participate in creating our stress. In fact, we are usually completely unaware of how our *reaction* to a situation exacerbates our stress. Think about how people react differently to the very same situation. For example, throwing a dinner party for twelve could be creative and fun for one person but nerve-racking for another. Living in a big city could be a thrilling rush for one person but an overwhelming nightmare for someone else.

Clearly some of us are wired to sustain a little more stimulation than others, but it's our minds themselves that really claim the power over how we react to potential stress. Imagine being stuck in traffic, late for a meeting. One person's heart rate rises as she goes into panic mode. Another person, as calm as the Dalai Lama himself, surrenders peacefully to whatever time he arrives. The event is neutral. Our response creates or reduces stress.

We all have our own personal internal and external stressors. Whenever I run stress management workshops, I always spend a few minutes letting people brainstorm about their own personal sources of stress—both the concrete circumstances in their lives and also the internal ruminations that wind them tight. Think for a moment about what factors cause you the most stress.

How much time and energy would you say gets absorbed by your reactions to stress? How many wasted hours, days, weeks, and years are consumed with your unproductive agitations? Most of us make ourselves literally sick from our responses to life. It's as if we float on the surface of life, caught in the choppy waves of circumstances. Little do we know that if we allowed ourselves to sink down, there would be a calm, quiet stillness completely undisturbed by the waves. The problem is that rather than taking a moment to sink to the blissful depth, we typically use our energies trying to tame the waves.

Stress Management

Wave taming is how many approaches to stress management work. Stress reduction programs offer concrete ways to create "outer peace" by changing outer circumstances (such as managing your time more effectively, going on vacation, keeping your keys in one spot, making sure your locks are secure) and/or offering specific ways to help your body manage stress (such as with diet, rest, and exercise). Although these lifestyle modifications can be extremely helpful, they don't lead, in and of themselves, to a sustained feeling of inner peace.

The problem is twofold. First, outer peace doesn't *necessarily* lead to inner peace. You could be lounging on a tropical beach but still be consumed with your to-do lists, worries, and resentments. You could be on the massage table but still wondering how many e-mails you've gotten in the past hour. And if you've ever tried traditional meditation, you know that you can be amidst deep silence and still have an overactive mind.

Second, the conditions of successful outer peace don't last. Sure, it's possible to relax and unwind with the proverbial bubble bath, but the relief is temporary. Needing outer peace in order to achieve sustained inner peace is a setup for eventual failure.

Believe me, I know. I have tried to create the perfect oasis of calm (when all five kids are out of the house). It works for a while. I am the female Buddha incarnate as I stroll through my silent, childless house and note each room staying perfectly organized from morning till night . . . that is, until my child army returns. Then I go from Buddha to berserk in sixty seconds flat.

When it comes to stress, we have to look at the difference between the stressors we can change and the stressors we can't. The popular Serenity Prayer speaks to this common wisdom:

> *God grant me the serenity to accept the things I cannot change, the courage to change the things I can, and the wisdom to know the difference.*

If we have a high-intensity, unsustainable lifestyle that can be changed, then it should be changed (like quitting a miserable job, moving to the quiet country, or leaving an abusive partner). However, more often, stress emerges in ways that we cannot change (we have a sick child, our house burned down, we were fired, the airplane was delayed for another hour, we have a houseful of children).

If we convince ourselves that inner peace is dependent on circumstances being just so, then bliss must be deferred until the one day when all the dust settles . . . when we go on vacation, when the kids are grown, when the big deal happens, when we retire. We live with a vision of life where peacefulness is *out there* somewhere. We either feel like we can't quite get there, or if we can, it slips away as quickly as it arrived.

Inner peace really is an inside job (they don't call it *inner* for nothing). The words of the great American Transcendentalist, Ralph Waldo Emerson, "What lies behind us and what lies before us are small matters compared to what lies within us," echo the words of Jesus, "The Kingdom of Heaven is within you." What this means to us is that the power of inner peace is available in each and every chaotic moment.

The Inner of Peace

When we reside in that place called peace, we have a full throttle experience of the present moment and therefore have no worries about a future and no hang-ups about a past. We also experience a deep measure of surrender or at least acceptance of "what is." In other words, there is no resistance, no control, no fighting reality. There is a relaxed and settled "yes" to life.

Can you remember ever feeling this way? Think of a time when you felt completely relaxed and at ease—either recently or long ago. Where were you? Was it day or night? How was the weather? Were you alone or with others? What were the sounds, tastes, smells of this moment of pure peace? Were you in nature, near water, in a forest? Were you a child? Was there music or perhaps the sounds of nature? Close your eyes for a moment, picture the details, and let the memory imprint itself in your mind.

As you recall this peaceful moment, you may remember feeling slightly more aligned with all of life. You may notice that your body relaxes, your mind feels less troubled, your heart opens, and your senses come into sharp focus.

I call this memory the "peace place," a visual reminder of your internal reservoir of serenity. It's a glimpse of the calm that lies below our everyday circumstances. You may have thought that your peace place experience was caused by the sunset, ocean waves, or silence, but these circumstances merely took you home to yourself. There is no doubt that the right environment can help to clear your mind and relax your body, but the true anchor of peace is found within you.

Through intentionally summoning a feeling of calm, we literally change the chemistry of our bodies by activating our parasympathetic nervous systems, which, in turn, creates more serenity in our bodies. So when we go to our peace place frequently, peace becomes a habit newly wired into our brains.

Fortunately, we can go there anytime—on a crowded subway platform, in the doctor's waiting room, in the grocery store line (in fact, going to this peace place is one of the Shortcuts, "Take Me Away"). We have the power to feel calm and centered in the midst of any raging storm.

One of my favorite quotes is:

Peace: It does not mean to be in a place where there is no noise, trouble, or hard work. It means to be in the midst of those things and still be calm in your heart.

—ANONYMOUS

What we're talking about here is a paradigm shift: moving away from our dependence on outer peace as a prerequisite for inner peace. Personally, I knew that I needed to internalize this message and put it into action because my old responses to the "stress" of a busy household were making me miss the pleasures of time with my children and my stepchildren. I knew that I had no one to blame but myself for sapping the joy out of living, casting shadows on my blessings.

Missing out on the wonder of my life was especially distressing given my perspective as a grief counselor. For two decades, I have watched grievers struggle with the loss of their children, spouses, parents, and siblings. Heartbroken and stunned by loss, grievers realize that the precious gift of life should never be taken for granted or, worse, squandered. So it felt particularly wasteful to have stress stand between me and the ability to fully savor my life.

Like so many, I had seen glimpses of inner peace (mostly on retreats and in silent places), so I knew the feeling was possible. But I couldn't depend on those few and far between moments. The right conditions happened too infrequently. I didn't want to be a "vacation" peaceful person. I wanted to live and breathe peace—to have it be my default setting. I knew the lake of calm was just below the surface . . . an inner spaciousness full of magic. But I still wasn't sure how to get there and how to stay there.

Then the Shortcuts came along to show me the way.

Shortcut Solutions

Sylvia sat across from me, clearly agitated. This forty-something woman—mother of two teenage boys, going through a divorce but still living under the same roof with her soon-to-be ex—crossed her denim-clad legs exclaiming, "I'm *soooo* stressed out!"

"Have you ever tried meditation?" I asked. This was a question that I usually asked clients at some point in our work together. Even though I hadn't been successful yet with a formal daily practice, I knew that the calming benefits of doing so were tremendous. As it turned out, regardless of whether my client was a stay-at-home mom, a working professional, or a retiree, I almost always got the same response.

"Ha!" she barked. "You know I don't have time for that!" She was a single mom with a full-time job, a house to run, and a to-do list that never ended. She really did seem too busy to meditate.

I knew that stress was no doubt taking its toll on her, so I persisted. "I could teach you techniques that you could do in three minutes, even one minute."

Sylvia responded slowly, "I have to be honest. Even if I had the time, I don't think I would do it. I've tried meditation and quite frankly, it's a little bit boring. When I close my eyes and sit quietly, my mind wanders. I just think of the million and one things I've got to do and I get even more stressed."

Hmm. I appreciated her honesty, but it wasn't the first time that I had heard a client (or a friend) suggest that meditation wasn't for them. That's when I realized that there should really be some exercises for nonmeditators that offered the same benefits achieved by lengthy meditations: stillness, calm, and a feeling of inner peace. What I really needed was a book for my clients—and myself, for that matter—that had short, informal, peace-inducing exercises that took virtually no time to implement.

I thought to myself, *We all manage to find the time to brush our teeth, don't we? We all have the time to wash our hands throughout the day, right?* There must be a way to weave some instant inner peace throughout the day while doing things that we're already doing.

"Well, let's see," I brainstormed. "What if we came up with something you could do to calm yourself that isn't a formal meditation?"

"Maybe . . ." she responded skeptically.

"And what if it was something to do while you were washing your hands or during some other routine activity?"

She smiled, then laughed. "That would be perfect!"

Sylvia left that session with a spontaneously created exercise ("Go with the Flow") to help her deal with her ongoing divorce proceedings.

Encouraged by her enthusiastic response, I began actively developing the Shortcuts. Some I had been using sporadically for years, others popped out at unexpected moments, sometimes waking me up at night. I kept a pad of paper and pen around me for these bursts of inspiration. They say that necessity is the mother of invention, and I realized that I needed these Shortcuts as much as my clients did.

I started sharing them with other clients and I was amazed at the positive responses. Often in the past, when I assigned an exercise of journaling, meditating, or keeping track of some behavior, my clients had a hard time complying. They would come into session with a hangdog look as they confessed that they hadn't done their "homework."

But with the Shortcuts, my clients' success rate skyrocketed. Why? Because even for someone with a busy lifestyle, the Shortcuts—accessible and simple to implement—quickly become habits.

I soon started offering community workshops on the Shortcuts and the response was equally enthusiastic. Basically, most of us who are frazzled, busy, and stressed are hungry for easy techniques that help us stay grounded and calm.

The Shortcuts

So, what are the Shortcuts? Like any "shortcut" in life, be it when you're driving or when you're cooking, these are direct routes, fast tracks to your goal that are easily integrated into your life. Specifically, the tools are quick things to do, think, say, or imagine to make you feel calmer, more relaxed, and less stressed. They're inspired by and drawn from the following tried-and-true healing techniques.

Cognitive-Behavioral Therapy—A psychotherapeutic approach that focuses on helping individuals learn new ways of thinking in order to change negative behaviors. Clients learn to watch their minds in action by developing the practice of observing and changing unskillful thoughts. Cognitive-behavioral therapy helps individuals track the connections between their thoughts, emotions, and behaviors.

Yoga—This Hindu-based healing discipline and spiritual practice is aimed at training the mind and body. Practiced for more than five thousand years, it combines breathing exercises, postures, and meditation. A few of the benefits of yoga include calming both the mind and the central nervous system, body awareness, and stress relief.

Spiritual Wisdoms and Practices—These techniques are collectively known to calm the mind and spirit as well as to open the heart. Furthermore, they cultivate a lifestyle that is based on forgiveness, nonviolence, and kindness.

~ *Mantra meditation/Centering prayer*—repeating meaningful words or phrases in a relaxed and still state

~ *Mindfulness*—a practice of nonjudgmental awareness of the moment, intentionally heightened focus on a single task

~ *Loving-kindness*—a practice of compassion and generosity toward oneself and others, known as *metta* in Eastern traditions and agape in Western traditions

~ *Equanimity*—a state of abiding calmness and composure even under stress, the practice of evenhanded responses to both "good" and "bad"

~ *Energy healing*—manipulating universal energy, or chi, within the body to raise vibrational frequencies and bring about balance

Visualization Therapy—A form of self-hypnosis that uses your imagination to summon the details of places and feelings, this technique harnesses the power of imagery to heal the mind and even elicit physiological changes in the body. Visualizations have been used successfully to deal with depression, chronic pain, epilepsy, self-confidence, and performance success.

Affirmation Therapy—This is a healing approach that focuses on positive self-talk. Affirmations work with the subconscious mind in order to change or replace unhealthy core belief systems. Affirmations are positive suggestions or statements that, when repeated frequently, can redirect ingrained patterns of negative thinking and retrain the mind toward a positive mental attitude. Affirmations have been used to address a wide range of problems including addictions, lack of self-confidence, stress, depression, and other psychological issues.

Positive Psychology—This approach veers away from the medical model of "pathology and cure" and instead emphasizes a positive image of humans as inherently healthy and competent. Positive psychology aims to help people intensify their happiness and find balance in their lives. It stresses the cultivation of gratitude, optimism, and inner strength. This approach empowers people to take a more active role in their own healing process.

Mind–Body Medicine—Based on the holistic perspective of integrative health, mind–body medicine is based on the premise that thoughts can affect the symptoms, functioning, and behaviors of the body. Current neuropsychological research emphasizes the plasticity of the brain and its ability to change. Repetitive experiences and thoughts can actually cause new neural pathways to develop in the brain.

At the Core

Regardless of the type of tool or its method of inspiration, the core experience of each Shortcut is that it creates a "pattern interrupt" to our unconscious reactions, thoughts, and behaviors. When we disrupt our thought stream, we create a gap in momentum. In that moment when autopilot pauses, we have a space for *awareness, redirection,* and *restoration.*

Awareness—Awareness is the key to seeing how our own minds perpetuate the cycle of stress in our lives. When we momentarily unhook from the spiral of activity, the Shortcuts help us gain an alertness, a present stillness, that grounds us in witnessing and experiencing the present moment. This clarity helps us savor our life with gratitude right as we're living it.

Redirection—When we pause in the midst of stress or conflict, the Shortcuts help us reorient, reframe, and redirect what is happening. They help us turn toward more positive energy and work to ingrain positive emotions in our brains. Most parents and educators instinctively know the tactic of redirection. Imagine the toddler who is frustrated with a broken toy and the kindergarten teacher who redirects him to the marvelously colored blocks . . . bliss.

Restoration—When we momentarily halt the relentless pace of daily living, the Shortcuts create a nourishing respite. The kind of pauses that we usually build into our daily patterns are often activities designed to "numb us out"—like drinking, smoking, watching television, surfing the Internet, recreational shopping, or playing video games. The pauses created by the Shortcuts actually calm our nervous systems and connect us to a greater whole.

In the midst of stressful lives, these specially designed moments here and there can actually wake us up to wonder, redirect us to peace, and restore our birthright of tranquility. Yes, we will still have challenges in our lives, but by using the Shortcuts, we change our relationship to the stress of those challenges. We will feel less reactive even though our circumstances remain unchanged. And, amazingly, by using the Shortcuts, we can actually rewire our nervous systems.

The Science of Shortcuts

Each of the Shortcuts in this book activates the parasympathetic nervous system (PNS), the regulatory and calming system of the body and mind. This wing of our nervous system handles the so-called rest-and-digest systems in our body. When the PNS is stimulated, it dampens the fight-or-flight systems in our body, lowers our blood pressure, helps us disengage from the external world, lifts our mood, strengthens our immune system, and generally helps our body recover from stress.

Neuroscientific research has confirmed that the brain is malleable, with a clear capacity to create new neural pathways in response to novel repetitive behaviors. The brain registers a new experience by connecting our neurons in ways that they hadn't been connected before. The more often we repeat the experience, the stronger the circuitry. In other words, simply responding to stress in a new and healthy way, over time, actually creates new, healthy habits that are wired into our brains.

The Shortcut System

Repetition, then, is key for a healthy habit to become ingrained. The problem, of course, is that most of us start with good intentions to eat right, exercise, meditate, but we don't keep it up. It's like having a bottle of megavitamins collecting dust at the back of the pantry. But consider what happens when we link taking our vitamins with eating our breakfast: The odds of remembering our vitamins are drastically increased. Sylvia was able to consistently use the "Go with the Flow" Shortcut because she paired it with the ordinary habit of washing her hands. This is the power of a trigger. The key to the Shortcut system is pairing the tools with existing habits.

Remember that habits are no more than established connections between neurons in our brains. When we intentionally respond to a trigger in a new way, new connections are formed and over time become stronger. Using thoughts, feelings, activities, and ordinary experiences in our daily lives to trigger Shortcuts, we develop new habits. And as habits, Shortcuts begin to happen automatically, "triggered" by the ordinary flow of our lives.

This isn't a new concept. In fact, you may already know several Shortcuts. Remember the scene from the beloved movie *The Sound of Music* in which Maria comforts the frightened children on a stormy night by singing of her "favorite things"? When she feels sad, she remembers some of her favorite things and no longer feels bad. The trigger: feeling sad. The tool: thinking of favorite things.

Or remember in the movie *The King and I* when Anna consoles her frightened son on the ship before they reach Siam? She tells him that whenever she feels afraid she whistles a happy tune. The trigger: fear. The tool: whistling.

Those two examples are based on emotional triggers, but the Shortcuts also work with a range of behavioral and experiential triggers. When you hear someone sneeze, what do you automatically do? Without even thinking, you say, "Bless you."

I once took an online class with a teacher who had studied with the preeminent Vietnamese monk, Thich Nhat Hanh. During the time of his study, a monk would wander through the monastery with a bell that he would ring at random times through the day. My teacher had been instructed to stop what he was doing whenever he heard the bell and take a moment of silence for mindful awareness.

This is another example of a trigger (bell) and a tool (mindful silence). Still to this day, whenever he hears the phone ring (his version of the monastery bell), he is triggered to take a mindful moment.

The Shortcuts system works for two important reasons:

1. The tools are simple and very effective.
2. The tools are linked to already existing triggers in your life.

Shortcuts are meant to happen so naturally that you can't help but use them. This was good news for me personally because I have a long history of knowing that certain activities are good for me (like exercise and long meditations) but just not having the time or the will to make them happen. When using the Shortcuts system of linking tools to triggers, I found that there *is* time.

Shortcuts to Inner Peace

So, let's get started! This book offers you seventy Shortcuts, each based on the "Tools and Triggers" system and is divided into two main sections: The Thread Basics and The Peace Portals. The Thread Basics section uses our routines, our frequent interactions with others, and our five senses as vehicles for finding peace. The Peace Portals section focuses on four key avenues that lead to your innate inner peace:

- *the body*—being calm, still, relaxed
- *the mind*—being unattached to thoughts, a witness, mindful
- *the heart*—being compassionate and grateful
- *the Spirit*—being connected to a larger energy, accepting, aligned

The appendices categorize the Shortcuts for easy reference. If you prefer "visualization" tools over "action" tools, for example, you can find them listed all together. You will also find tools grouped by specific needs, such as when you feel stressed or when you are angry, and by specific triggers, such as when you pay your bills.

So that you don't get overwhelmed, I suggest working with one or two Shortcuts at a time. Spend a few weeks getting each one settled into your lifestyle and then try adding another one. It takes approximately three weeks of consistent use for a habit to become ingrained.

Or you might want to experiment briefly with different Shortcuts until you decide which ones you want to "adopt" in your life. You may find that you gravitate easily and quickly to one tool or type of tool but that others don't work at all for you. That's fine. Go with what feels right. In twelve-step recovery programs, there is an expression, "Take what you want and leave the rest." This philosophy applies to the Shortcuts as well.

The most helpful tip I can offer is to use notes as reminders to yourself. If you're going to work with "Morning Glories," for example, a tool triggered by brushing your teeth, then keep a note next to your toothbrush for several weeks. If you're going to work with "Rest in Peace," triggered by putting your head on the pillow to go to sleep, then keep a note on your bedside table.

Put notes on bathroom mirrors, car dashboards, by your computer, on kitchen cabinets. Let the notes cue you to do the Shortcuts until they gel as natural habits. Once they become integrated in your lifestyle, you won't be able to remember life without them.

When I was growing up, *The Wizard of Oz* was one of my favorite movies. Okay, yes, the flying monkeys did freak me out, but I was mesmerized by Dorothy and her pals. As virtually everyone knows, Dorothy wanted to go home but she didn't know how to get there. She took a long journey to meet the Wizard, thinking he could help her, but in fact he couldn't.

What Dorothy didn't know was that she actually had the means to return home via the magic contained within her ruby red slippers. She wore those shoes night and day but never knew the power that they contained. Only when she was instructed by Glinda the Good Witch did she learn how to use them to her advantage.

We are not unlike Dorothy in that we have incredibly powerful portals to inner peace, but mostly we don't even know that we have them, much less how to use them. This book shows how our daily patterns, our relationships, and our senses along with our bodies, minds, hearts, and spirits are just waiting to lead us to a place of deep peace and pure serenity. Consider this book a little like Glinda—it will show you what to do, offering easy instructions on how to get where you want to go: home to yourself. Get ready to feel grounded and peaceful no matter what your circumstances, your health, your past, or your future. Inner peace (a deep abiding stillness) is our natural birthright, and using the Shortcuts regularly and consistently will create a fabric of well-being that awakens deep levels of joy. Then, at the end of our lives, we'll look back and know that we did more than just struggle to survive: We savored life more fully and were awakened to the miracles.

The Thread Basics

Your Daily Thread

Shortcuts to Weave Through Your Day

When I was a kid, one of the big vacations that I remember was going to Colonial Williamsburg. I was mesmerized by the realistic slice of eighteenth-century life: people walking around in period clothing . . . hat shops . . . blacksmith studios . . . marbled paper.

But one store that I remember in particular was the Textile Shoppe. In the back room, a woman sat hunched over a large loom and there she painstakingly wove one thread at a time across the vast wooden structure. One simple thread at a time.

Sure enough, as time went by, each thread built upon the one before it until a solid cloth began to materialize. It seemed like magic to me. My mother had to tear me away from watching this slow-motion progress.

A single strand seemed like nothing, and yet somehow,

woven in one after another, a fabric was born. Imagine each Shortcut as a thread that weaves itself through our days and weeks creating a texture of peacefulness.

Obviously, for both weaving and daily habits, consistency and repetition are vital to success. One thread alone won't create a fabric, just like one vitamin or one exercise class won't make us healthy. If we are to see the benefits of any healthy regime, we must give our new habits time to become imprinted; we must make them a regular part of our lives.

This section offers a basic daily template of ten triggers and ten corresponding tools. It's a sample of how you could use the tools throughout an average day.

Feel free to customize the Shortcuts with personal triggers that fit your own unique schedule. Modify them, tweak them, craft them to fit your life. For example, a woman in one of my workshops realized that "Morning Glories," a Shortcut that I suggest while brushing your teeth, was better triggered for her when she was making her bed in the morning.

Another woman realized that riding the elevator to work was a perfect opportunity for a Shortcut. She devised her own as she imagined stress falling off of her as she "flew" up each floor. Make the Shortcuts your own.

Build one upon another, creating a sturdy daily fabric of well-being. If one new habit has the power to change your life, imagine what a day of new habits can do!

TRIGGER: In the morning just before getting out of bed.

TOOL: As you lie in bed, state an affirmation as a form of mindful intention. Begin with a deep breath. As you breathe out, say, "I am peaceful today" or "I experience inner peace throughout my day." Say it in the present tense as if it is already happening and let yourself feel that peace sink down deep inside you. Find a phrase that is meaningful to you. You could also try one of the following: "I choose peace today," "Every day has joy," or "I radiate peace." Think of this Shortcut as a morning vitamin, your "peace pill." Allow yourself the habit of starting your day with a specific peaceful intention, every day.

My sister once sent me an e-mail questionnaire that consisted of a series of silly and playful questions. She had answered the questions and was seeking my answers to the same questions. In fact, I had gotten this same survey from quite a few cyberspace friends!

The questions allowed for humorous interpretations, depending on the wit of the respondent. One question that stuck in my memory was: *What is your first thought in the morning?* My sister wrote: *If it's a weekend, "Yippee"; if it's a weekday, "Yuck!"* My response to the same question was, *Did I get enough sleep?* Being a frequent insomniac, sleep was a habitual concern.

It dawned on me that the first few thoughts of the day are powerful directives. When you're in that fuzzy haze between sleep and wakefulness, thoughts sink in with a hypnotic potency. Thoughts like *Ugh, how will I ever get through my crazy day?* don't get you started on a peaceful note.

But thoughts that are intentionally designed to foster peacefulness . . . well, those thoughts are worth keeping. Your first thoughts do matter; they set the stage not only for your day but for your life. Sound dramatic? Try it and see for yourself.

PURPOSE: *When we take a moment to set our intention on calm, we set the day off on a trajectory of peacefulness and we break the cycle of automatic morning thoughts. Over time, a new pattern becomes fixed in our brains. We can begin to create an intentional life of inner peace with our very first thought of the day.*

MORNING GLORIES

TRIGGER: When brushing your teeth in the morning.

TOOL: As you brush your teeth in the morning, think of three things that you will be facing in your day. Don't identify them as *good* or *bad, fun* or *stressful*; simply identify them neutrally and imagine that you will be open to them as experiences, much as a morning glory opens to the sun. Say, "Today I will be open to the meeting with curiosity," "Today I will be open to the class with curiosity," or "Today I will be open to the phone conference with curiosity." As you encounter the three things during your day, remember to be open and curious. Perhaps you'll need to exclaim, "Oh! *This* is how it's going to unfold today!" Optionally, you could identify three positive qualities (rather than three events) that you will to be receptive to, such as love, patience, or abundance.

My children's kindergarten teacher, besides being a gifted educator, had a not-so-secret talent: She was a marvelous photographer. She entered local competitions, often winning. Best of all, if she happened to send you a card for one reason or another, it usually included one of her beautiful nature photos taped to heavy card stock. I was so moved by one of her pictures of sun-drenched blue morning glories that I framed the 4 × 6 photograph and hung it in my bathroom.

One morning while I was groggily brushing my teeth, I found myself running through my to-do list of the day: "Got that business meeting downtown." *Ugh.* "Got that client with the difficult circumstances." *Ugh.* "Got that lunch with a friend." *Yeah.* "Gotta pick up kids from three directions tonight." *Okay.* "Got that rehearsal tonight." *Fun but will be too tired . . . ugh.* I noticed that I had an automatic tendency to label each activity as *good* or *bad.* I had a grit-my-teeth-and-bear-it attitude as I prepared to muscle through my day.

Then my eyes came to rest on the morning glories photograph. I thought about how these beautiful flowers open each morning, fresh and optimistic to take in a new day. They don't label, discriminate, judge . . . they simply open and receive.

"I want to be like a morning glory," I pronounced. Then and there I decided to give it a try. Not only did I attempt to remain nonjudgmental about my day's activities as I reviewed them over toothpaste, I tried to be curious and receptive throughout the day. And guess what? It worked.

PURPOSE: *When we start our days with receptivity, we automatically create an energy of nonresistance. Remembering our morning glories as the day unfolds, we redirect our minds to positive emotions and begin to cultivate a feeling of curiosity and acceptance. This open attitude is fodder for inner peace.*

CATCH AND RELEASE

TRIGGER: When taking a shower.

TOOL: Think of your three top worries—the things that stress you or that you're dreading. "Catch" each negative thought, name it as a worry, fear, judgment, or complaint, and imagine it in the suds. "Release" each one into the water and down the drain. Say, for example, "I release and wash away my fear of a bad performance review at work today" or "I release and wash away my worry about my daughter driving." Release it to the current of life and trust it to go with the flow.

I have never been much of a fisherwoman, but when I was a young child, my grandfather took me and my sister on a boat for a fishing adventure. Barbie-wielding little girls that we were, we never did get the hang of putting worms on a hook. We enjoyed playing in the tackle box, but the actual act of hauling up a fish fighting for its life, and then gutting it, didn't exactly excite either one of us.

When I was an adult, I tried fly-fishing—once—but it didn't go over so well. I was in my first trimester of a pregnancy and I felt so nauseous that I nearly collapsed in the river. But I was intrigued by the concept of catch and release. Although it was a more humane way to fish, I would hardly say that the poor fish was left unharmed after a ferocious battle and return to his habitat. I imagined an underground support group of battle-scarred bass and rainbow trout, some with hooks still in their mouths, comparing trauma stories.

Still the idea of catch and release is a useful concept for our thoughts. Most of our entrenched negative and fretful thoughts serve absolutely no purpose other than whipping us into a nervous frenzy. They can begin to act as a poison to our well-being. But once we release them we improve our ability to think clearly, make decisions, take action, and enjoy ourselves.

The shower, already a relatively relaxing place with warm water splashing on the body, is a perfect place to "catch" polluting thoughts and "release" them into the stream. Let them flow out of your mind and into the river of life. Most things we obsess about are completely beyond our control. Release them and free yourself of their burden.

PURPOSE: *As we increase our awareness of our negative thoughts, they begin to lose their strength. When we let go of negative energy that occupies the mind and spirit, we restore ourselves to a state of calm.*

FREEZE FRAME

TRIGGER: For all beverage breaks.

TOOL: As you take your first sip of a morning beverage, stop for a moment, take a deep breath, freeze the frame (make a mental or audible camera *click* sound), and think, *Life is good.* As you take your first sip of your lunch drink, your afternoon coffee, your evening drink, create the habit of stopping to take a mental snapshot. Feel the liquid go down your throat. Notice, breathe, absorb, and savor the tastes as well as the moment. Imprint on your mind the happiness habit of noting to yourself, *Ah, this is a good moment.*

When I was in college, I had the great fortune to spend my junior year in London, England. It was a fascinating year in most regards, full of adventures that felt fresh in ways that only twenty-year-olds can experience. Walking down a crowded street and riding the underground subway (affectionately called the Tube) were thrilling adventures for me.

Having never lived in an urban environment before, I was fascinated by the many sights and sounds of big-city living. But one curious association that I have with England is the complete enthusiasm—nay, near worship—that the English have for their *beverages.*

The Brits are, of course, known for their abiding affection for tea of all varieties, but they have equal enthusiasm for their blackberry juice, cold colas, and pints at the pub. Yet it wasn't just the mere consumption of liquids that struck me. It was the ritual, the courtship, the rapture. Whether it was the "ah" reaction to that first sip of tea perfectly mixed with sugar and cream or the reverent first encounter with the foam on the top of a pint of ale, I thought to myself again and again, *These people know how to appreciate their beverages.*

If you're old enough to remember the Lipton "plunge" advertisements from the 1970s, you'll remember that sense of "ahhhhhhhhhhh" as the happy tea drinker fell backward in a pool of cool water, refreshed and satisfied with a glass of iced tea.

Multiple times a day we have just such an opportunity for complete satisfaction . . . if we remember to stop, notice, and savor. Every first sip can be a moment of inner refreshment, of utter delight. So swirl your beverage as a fine-wine connoisseur would do in a tasting, open your senses to the experience, take your mental *click*, and give thanks for the nectar. "Ah, this is living."

PURPOSE: *This tool helps train our minds to focus on a moment of simple pleasure. It identifies a happy moment and holds it in our consciousness, creating an imprint of positive experience. It cultivates gratitude, a quality highly correlated with peacefulness. Finally, it creates a "pause" which momentarily stops the physical and emotional spiral of the day.*

STOP, DROP, AND ROLL

TRIGGER: When stopped at a red light.

TOOL: "Stop," "drop" down into your heart, and "roll" out
a little goodwill to your fellow travelers. Look at the people
in other cars in front of you, behind you, passing around
you, and recognize that each one of them is just like you:
They want happiness and they want to be free from suffering. To each person you focus on say or think something
like:

> *May you know happiness.*
> *May you be free from suffering.*
> *Peace be with you.*
> *I hope you have a nice day.*

When I was a kid, we had a station wagon with a backseat that faced
the back window of the car. So, if you happened to be sitting in the
backseat, you actually looked directly at the cars behind you. Back
in the day, most station wagons had this design feature.

Recently, I was having a stressful day, preoccupied with my
thoughts and worries. As I was driving, I came to a stoplight
behind an old-fashioned station wagon, and lo and behold, there
were two small children in the backseat facing me. I must admit

that it's a bit unnerving at first to be face-to-face with someone at a stoplight when you are not accustomed to making eye contact.

I smiled at the children and the next thing I knew they were waving at me. Then I held up the peace sign, which they mimicked. The three of us laughed, and then the little girl blew me a kiss, which I returned. We were having such a love-fest that I actually felt a little sad when the light turned green. Those few moments of goodwill had changed my day—my heart felt lifted.

What a nice way to spend a pause at a red light, I thought. Most of us spend red lights either in unconsciousness, fretting about the future or the past, or grumbling at the driver who wasn't going fast enough. *Why not use red lights to wish a little goodwill to others?* I mused.

Imagine if at every stoplight every person in every car was having thoughts of goodwill and kindness. Imagine if at every stoplight every person was aware, even for a moment, of their compassion for others. My prediction: Road rage would cease! We would have a very different world indeed.

Use this Shortcut to actually look at the people in the cars around you and remember for a moment that they have loved ones, jobs, worries, delights, fears, joys, and entire lives, just like you do. Connect for a brief moment and wish them well.

PURPOSE: *This tool "quenches the fire" of road rage by getting us out of our own little worlds. Commuting for many people can be the most stressful time in their workdays. Actively using this Shortcut gives us another way to be in the car. It opens us to our surroundings, expanding our sense of self by connecting with others who also wish for happiness and wish to be free from suffering. Warm feelings toward others activate the calming aspects of our own nervous systems. Opening our hearts with compassion, we experience a deeper sense of inner peace.*

GO WITH THE FLOW

TRIGGER: **When washing your hands.**

TOOL: **Whenever you're at a sink and touch water, let the stream of warm liquid cue you to say, "Go with the flow" or "I trust the universe" or "Everything is as it should be." This reminds you to** *let go* **and flow with the current of life.**

Most of us like to believe that we're in control, master of our fates. The cold hard truth, however, is that we actually control very little in our lives. We can't control other people, the weather, death, sickness, delays, traffic, long lines in stores, and on and on. We do most everything we can to keep up the pretense of our in-charge personas, but somewhere deep inside we suspect it's all an illusion. Nowhere is this more evident than during air travel.

Now I don't spend a lot of time in airplanes, but I have flown enough through the years to experience nine hour delays, canceled flights, closed airports, equipment malfunctions, de-icing, screaming infants (once it was my own), kicking children (directly behind me), cramped middle seats, turbulence, and vomiting neighbors. I've been on short flights, long flights, small planes, and jumbo jets. All I can say is that it's a humbling experience because you can control absolutely *nothing* except your personal state of mind (and usually that feels beyond your control as well).

One summer afternoon, I was in an airport and an airline employee came over the public address system to announce that our flight was delayed indefinitely until a thunderstorm system moved through Denver. Much to my surprise, a teenage boy sitting next to his mother across from me got up in a rage, yelled at the top of his lungs "DAMN!" and began kicking a nearby wheelchair (which, fortunately, was empty). The mother of the irate teen looked mortified but didn't say a single word to her son. People all around me began huffing, whipping out their cell phones, and muttering similar obscenities under their collective breaths.

I too was starting to feel my blood pressure rise, but then I had a strange sort of out-of-body experience. I "clicked" and suddenly became a detached observer, like I was watching an airport-delay scene in a movie theater. I watched the would-be passengers responding with frustration, some yelling at the airline employees (as if that would cause the storm system to move faster). I realized how laughably absurd the situation appeared. They were like a bunch of toddlers throwing tantrums because their recess was rained out.

Within seconds, I clicked back into my body. With my eyes closed, I envisioned the rains that were responsible for our delays, and I just "let go." I imagined the waters drenching me and in my head began to chant, *Go with the flow.* With that, I calmly opened my book and proceeded to have a great read for the next couple of hours while I waited for all the storms to pass.

It has been said that whenever we fight with reality, we lose. Learning to accept what's already happening, rolling with the

TRIGGER: When using the bathroom (a time when you have a moment to yourself).

TOOL: Breathe in through your nose to the count of five. Feel the air as it comes through your nose and expands into your lungs. Hold your breath to the count of five. Exhale through your mouth to the count of at least five (longer is even better). Upon exhaling, purse your lips as if blowing through a straw. Repeat several times.

I went through a brief phase with my kids when I was trying to teach them to meditate. Before we went out for the school bus, we had what I called SSS (Sixty Seconds of Silence). I rang a bell at which point we all closed our eyes, sat in silence for sixty seconds, and then I rang the bell again to close our meditation.

My elementary school–aged kids were initially good sports. They'd shift around a bit, cough and occasionally open their eyes in exasperation, but by and large, they were willing to indulge in this strange morning habit. One day, my first-grader told me that the sixty seconds were just too boring and she needed something to do in that minute.

Aha. Lots of adults also feel that meditation is too boring. Who wants to be left alone with their crazy, boring thoughts, after all?

So I thought about a breathing technique that I learned from a colleague, known as the 4-7-8 breath (inhale to the count of four, hold to the count of seven, and exhale to the count of eight). It is described and widely recommended by Dr. Andrew Weil, but I've also seen it suggested in t'ai chi communities. The 4-7-8 breathing technique is recommended for stress reduction, as it acts as a natural tranquilizer on the central nervous system. I modified that breathing technique to 5-5-5 because it felt more balanced and I thought it would be easier for my kids to remember.

Even the 5-5-5 was too long for the many mornings that we sprinted out the door to catch the school bus. And eventually, as the kids got older, they whined about the practice and it fell out of use. Oh well, at least I planted a seed for them and who knows when it might sprout into growth!

PURPOSE: *Breath work is universally considered grounding, relaxing, and physically invigorating. Deep exhalations stimulate calming mechanisms in our bodies. Holding air briefly in the lungs also creates elasticity and flexibility, leading to better overall health. When we redirect our minds to an awareness of our breath, we create a moment of calm in which inner peace can bloom.*

TRIGGER: When you get in the car or before you get on public transportation.

TOOL: Look to the sky . . . contemplate the vast space, details in the clouds, the colors, imagine beyond the blue sky to our solar system and even beyond that. Imagine our galaxy as one of hundreds of billions of galaxies (really!). "Breathe" in the sky, "breathe" in the spaciousness, and then exhale slowly. Say, "The spaciousness above is mirrored within me."

I have always been rather partial to sky miracles. I have frequently been moved to tears by sunrises, sunsets, cloud formations, starlit nights, falling stars, full moons, moon slivers, meteor showers, and lunar eclipses. The sky seems to be the perfect canvas for nature's artwork.

I have also enjoyed looking up to see silhouetted tree branches, colorful leaves, flocks of geese, butterflies, and other airborne beauties. There's just something about the sky that pulls my gaze upward. Perhaps that's why I have a special fondness for going up and into the sky.

The first time I ever went up in an airplane, I was thirteen years old and had just gotten my ears pierced (the ear piercing had nothing to do with the plane ride, but I still maintain the association). My family was going on a vacation and my sister and I were alert with excitement. We had gotten special stickers and books just for the plane ride. The stewardess (yes, they were stewardesses back then) brought us playing cards and wing pins. It was a grand adventure.

As it turns out, that day was a cloudy one, and I was unprepared for what awaited me above the clouds. It was a spectacular experience, rising through the clouds and emerging above the haze where, to my surprise, the day was clear and sunny. It seemed so extraordinary: cloudy day to sunny day in just a few moments. Even now, on rainy days, I look heavenward and know that the sun is shining above beautiful, puffy clouds, even if I cannot see it.

So, look up, encounter the sky, and reflect on its vast mysteries and surprises. How many of us ever take the time to just look *up*? We are so focused on looking down, forward, or backward that we forget about the vastness above us. Take this moment to focus your attention up and out to the universe, reminding yourself that life is bigger than the gerbil wheel of your to-do list and your racing mind. Remember that you are part of the expansiveness.

PURPOSE: *Deep exhalations stimulate a calming response in our bodies. This Shortcut allows a larger sense of spaciousness, which reflects the spaciousness within us. With it, we remind ourselves that we are a tiny and vital piece to the puzzle of our solar system, that most of our daily affairs are pretty "small stuff."*

SHAKEDOWN

TRIGGER: When coming home at the end of the day (or when transitioning out of a stressful situation).

TOOL: Before you walk through the door, spend a moment "shaking down" your body, as if you are shaking off water. Shake your right leg and foot, then your left leg and foot. Shake your right arm and hand; shake your left arm and hand. Gently shake your head and let your shoulders relax. Finish with a little twist of your torso to shake off any remaining energy from your day. Take a deep breath and heave a hearty sigh (a prolonged exhalation).

I'm a planner, so you can probably count on two hands the times that I displayed spontaneity. My children will remember the time that I unexpectedly stopped on a summer day for a round of miniature golf. They also like to recount when I made an impromptu stop at a local restaurant for tiramisu. And recently, in the *pouring* rain, I agreed to leave our cozy home to go for a neighborhood walk.

We suited up in jackets, rain boots, and took our beloved senior golden retriever for a *Singin' in the Rain* adventure. I have to admit that we had fun, although we all managed to get soaking wet (or maybe that was why we had fun). When we came back home, entering through the basement, we dropped our soggy coats in a heap. Just as I approached good old Hickory with a towel . . . yep . . . he made that big dog shake, that full body twist—as if in slow motion—and droplets flew through the air.

Wouldn't it be nice, I thought (after my shrieks subsided), *if we could all shake off things so efficiently?* Imagine if we could leave behind the workday—the meetings, e-mails, projects, errands, arguments with clients, meeting with the boss, the mess—leave all that behind as we enter our evening. What a relief that would be!

If we could leave the day in the past where it belongs, we could actually relax into the evening and be more present with our loved ones or with our nighttime activities. This Shortcut helps us do just that. We shake off our unwanted energy and clear ourselves so that our minds aren't preoccupied by the day. Then when we show up for our evening, we can really enjoy ourselves.

PURPOSE: *Relaxing our limbs sends a ripple effect of calm through our bodies. When we clear or shake off energy from our days, we restore ourselves to a place of calm so that we can be present as we transition from work to home.*

TRIGGER: When falling asleep.

TOOL: As you are in bed starting to fall asleep, review your day and list three things that happened for which you are grateful. Don't just vaguely remember each instance, but actively recall it and re-create the experience of it. Hold the feeling and think of yourself as a sponge, absorbing the memory in your body.

When I was growing up, every Christmas season we watched *White Christmas* starring Danny Kaye and Bing Crosby. During one classic scene, Bing's love interest, Rosemary Clooney, had a little trouble sleeping and went to the lodge in search of a late-night snack. She and Bing ended up sitting cozily by a fire while he crooned to her about counting your blessings before you fall asleep.

Sure, who wouldn't sleep better with Bing softly singing into their ears? But recalling things from the day to be grateful for is the next best thing. I used to try this technique with my children as I put them to bed. I would say, "Tell me something nice that happened today." This was a method for learning a little more about their day and helping them develop the habit of connecting with moments of joy in their life.

One night, my youngest daughter, Victoria, who had gotten

sick that day at school, told me that nothing nice had happened the whole day. Many of us might lay our heads on the pillow at night and think just that: There's *nothing* to be thankful for. I told her to think small, think simply: Wasn't she grateful to be in her own bed? Wasn't she grateful that there was medicine to bring down her fever? Wasn't it nice that she could rest on the couch and watch Disney movies today?

If you're having trouble thinking of blessings in your life, look for the simplest of details: something beautiful in nature, a smile from a friend, or that you have the use of your legs and arms. Every day has some "nice" things in it; make it your practice to notice three of them every night.

PURPOSE: *This tool is a way of focusing our minds on positive emotions. Joy can be described as "vibrant peace." By reflecting on moments of joy during our days, energy generates, and we become increasingly more joyful and more peaceful. Cultivating this evening gratitude practice will definitely help us sleep better!*

Shall We Dance?

Shortcuts to Weave Through Your Relationships

When I turned forty, I had a ten-, an eight-, and a six-year-old at home. To celebrate my big birthday, I decided to use the entire month for festivities. During that time, I had a small party; I went out for a fancy dinner with my husband; and, for my biggest gift of all, I gave myself the gift of a silent retreat weekend in a monastery.

Heaven! Silence was the thing that I most craved. There in my own little "hermitage" (a cottage bedroom/kitchenette), I spent three days in utter blissful silence. Four daily worship services (optional for me, mandatory for the monks) were the only exception to the rule of silence. I attended most of them.

Gregorian-style chants. Incense. Silence. A tiny little hut to temporarily call home. I felt like I was in another world. In fact, I *was* in another world! There were no little darlings around asking me for anything, no one to put to sleep at night. Was that a phone call to return? Nope. Nothing. My cell phone was to receive emergency calls only, and thankfully there were none.

You might think that I got bored with such an abundance of solitude, but I didn't. I spent time journaling, meditating, walking in the October woods. I spent time reading spiritual materials. I actually rested on a hammock and daydreamed for two entire hours. I napped. I reflected on forty years of living.

My meals with the brothers were the triple highlights of each day. To begin with, the monks were masterful chefs! The food was absolutely delicious. (Happily, they weren't an ascetic community.) During each lovely meal we sat, a handful of monks and me, at three different tables in a low-ceilinged room, dining in perfect conversation-free silence.

The cutlery clinked. The sounds of chewing and swallowing magnified. I looked separately at each brother, wondering what constellation of events led them to choose this blissful lifestyle. Our eyes met, locked, and crinkled in silent smiles.

And then my retreat was over. I packed up my things, grateful for such a heavenly respite and got in my car to drive home. Almost immediately upon pulling out of the monastic grounds, the world conspired to stress me out!

Why was everyone driving so quickly? Did that woman actually cut me off? Is that man riding my bumper? *Humph.* When I got home, it was like an avalanche of energy fell upon me. Children asking me for things, husband with a to-do list, phone calls and e-mails to return, client calls, messy house, a chorus of "What's for dinner?"

You've got to be kidding me. My celestial silence-induced peace popped like a bubble. My calm was being replaced by chaos. The afterglow hadn't even lasted an hour. *I can be peaceful on my own,* I thought angrily. *It's* them . . . *all of* them *who get in my way and ruin it.*

I guess you could say that my peace had been skin deep—not exactly enlightenment. The Buddha's story is somewhat different. They say that after seven years of searching, he sat beneath a bodhi tree to meditate until he reached enlightenment. He encountered visions that tempted him off the path, but he stayed the course. Eventually, it is said, he saw the true nature of all reality, thus attaining lasting inner peace.

One of the things he discovered, which subsequently became a central teaching in Buddhism, was the concept that we are all connected. In other words, our sense of separation from others is an illusion. When you harm someone, you harm yourself. When you wish them loving-kindness, it returns to you. We are all connected in a web of interdependence beyond even our ability to fathom.

Over time, I have come to realize that my own inner peace is impossible without learning to have peace with and around people. In fact, the people who appear to throw off my inner peace the most are precisely my best teachers about inner peace!

My stepchildren take karate, and I'm always impressed by the martial arts practice of bowing to your opponent before you begin a confrontation. The implicit message is to respect your "enemy," to thank him or her for whatever lessons are sure to be learned on the mat, and to trust the process that we all have something to learn from each other.

I believe that all people known and unknown are part of my equation for peace. Feeling joined with others leads to a deeper sense of rootedness and a vaster sense of inclusion.

The dance of relationships is a basic daily opportunity for cultivating inner peace because the personal relationships in our lives can help us grow, help us heal, and help us become better people. The tools in this section are designed for us to harness the power of relationships.

The first tool, "Mirror, Mirror on the Wall," starts with the most important relationship of all: the one you have with yourself. The next several tools are designed to help you improve existing loving relationships. And the rest of the tools in this section use some typically "sticky" interactions as avenues toward inner peace.

Do I still love to go on silent retreats? Definitely. But I can't depend on them to find my center. Fortunately, I have lots of opportunities with family, friends, and strangers to find that place over and over again.

Mirror, Mirror on the Wall

TRIGGER: **When standing in front of a mirror.**

TOOL: **Look at your reflection and say simply, "I accept all of you." For some people, "I forgive you," "I love you deeply and unconditionally," or "You are doing the best you can and I admire you for that" also work well. If nothing else, give yourself a vote of encouragement with a "hang in there."**

When I turned forty, I fulfilled my dream of "returning to the stage." Okay, I hadn't been on stage in a musical production since high school . . . and I had only been in the chorus . . . but still, the stage was calling me back.

And so I auditioned for a local community theater production of a British musical called *Honk!*, the story of the Ugly Duckling. I was, miraculously, cast as the lead mother duck. The classic coming-of-age tale recounts the journey of an outcast duckling growing up into his glory as a gorgeous swan.

At one point during his adventures, he meets a wise bullfrog who sings a song about accepting yourself, warts and all. The frog advises the young swan to trust himself, love himself and that in time, others will too.

What a nugget of wisdom, really. Don't we all need a wise little bullfrog around to remind us that we're beautiful as is? Self-loathing is probably one of the most common afflictions in our society . . . and how painfully unnecessary. Many of the kindest people are hateful, critical, and judgmental toward themselves.

Learning how to love ourselves can be a lifelong journey. This Shortcut invites us to begin that process of reversing self-hatred or self-criticism with a firm look in the eye and a kind word to ourselves. We are all unique expressions of this beautiful world with the innate capacity to love and be loved. We can listen for the inner critic and silence that voice with self-acceptance.

For some, this Shortcut will not feel like a stretch. It will merely be another way to experience love. In the end, we are handicapped in our ability to give love to others if we cannot first give love to ourselves. Let the mirror cue you to the habit of being kind to yourself.

PURPOSE: *When we train ourselves for self-acceptance and self-love, we build our sense of self-worth and break the habits of self-criticism. Using this Shortcut every day, we begin to disable the neural pathways of negativity in our brains. In remembering our own deeper truths, we open our hearts to inner peace.*

TRIGGER: When you find yourself annoyed with a loved one.

TOOL: Hum the song "You Are My Sunshine" and remember that your time together on this earth is limited. Recollect a time of joy with this person and let it fill the space of annoyance in your mind.

In 1988, as a student intern in a family counseling center, I sat with my first psychotherapy client. Although it seemed as if I should feel nervous, awkward even, instead it felt perfectly natural. I had been informally listening to and counseling people for years. I found it easy to ask the questions that others were reluctant to voice.

As it turns out, this first client was grieving the death of her sister who had been brutally murdered. What I didn't know at the time was that bereavement would become my professional specialty and that I would spend the next several decades hearing hundreds of stories of loss.

I have sat with a woman whose husband dropped dead at work, leaving her with three small children to raise. I have sat with a man whose son was tragically killed during a freak accident at the local elementary school. I have sat with a woman who watched her baby lose her long fight against leukemia.

Recently, I sat with a young woman whose father had died unexpectedly in his sleep . . . ten years previously. What she was struggling with was the fact that the night before he died, when she was teenager, they had had an argument. He had made a comment pressuring her to take more of an interest in her school-work and she had responded in a typical teen sassy manner. What she didn't expect, of course, was that he would die that night.

She had spent the last ten years feeling guilty about their last tense, even hostile, encounter. Not only had she been cheated of the chance to say good-bye (a frequent lament of those whose loved ones die suddenly), but she then had to live with the burden of her final memories.

How many times do we get annoyed with the very people we love the most? Isn't it easy to sweat the small stuff—the toilet seat left up, the socks on the floor, the dirty dishes left in the living room? And isn't it foolish to do so given that every single aspect of our lives together is incredibly fragile and temporary?

When I was pregnant with my first child, I used to sing to my growing belly "You Are My Sunshine." We pretty much all know the lyrics of this 1940 song, credited to Jimmie Davis and Charles Mitchell. But have you ever really listened to the words? Though it is a sweet song, it is quite sad too. It's a song about potential loss and unexpressed love. When I sang to my unborn child, I changed the penultimate line to "You'll *always* know, dear, how much I love you." But I still didn't want my sunshine to be taken away.

I hum this song to myself now as a reminder that my loved ones will be taken away from me one day (if I'm not taken first). And I want them to know how much I love them, even when I get momentarily annoyed by them.

PURPOSE: *Awareness of mortality is a gift if we use it to notice, to be appreciative, and to live fully. Against the backdrop of death, we see the small stuff for what it is, and therefore we are free to enrich our relationships.*

LOVE LETTERS

TRIGGER: When you have a pen in your hand—writing a to-do list, adding to your grocery list, or writing down messages from your voice mail.

TOOL: Make it a habit to give a little supportive note to someone every day. Write a few words of gratitude or appreciation, such as *Thanks for helping me empty the dishwasher this morning* or *Good luck on your test today*. Put them on mirrors, in lunch boxes, on computer screens, on dashboards, on desks, on pillows. Consider giving them to people you live with, people you work with, and friends and relatives. Paper the world with your love.

I will never forget my boss at my first big job. She was in her midthirties, but she seemed old and wise compared to the naïve twenty-two-year old pup that I was. She ran our department in a large New York City PR firm with a confident deftness. But most impressive and perhaps most memorable was her extreme thoughtfulness.

Almost every day she sent out "love notes" to her colleagues, subordinates, bosses, and clients. I know this because I actually *typed* her correspondence. (How did we live before computers?) The notes were short but kind:

> *Congratulations on your . . . promotion, new home,*
> *engagement, the new baby.*
> *Good luck with your . . . concert, marathon, big*
> *game.*
> *Great job on the . . . new campaign, press release,*
> *presentation.*
> *I'm thinking about you . . . when you adopt your*
> *baby, since you lost your father, during your*
> *surgery.*

And on and on. She also, daily, left handwritten notes on people's desks as well.

You might say that she was simply a good "player," that every note was a calculated motivation tool or ladder-climbing device. You could suggest that this was a tactic straight from Management Skills 101: Ply your employees with supportive notes and they will perform better. But I watched her and listened to her, and I could tell that her words were genuinely heartfelt. If you looked directly into her eyes, you saw warmth and compassion, not cold manipulation.

She inspired me. She taught me by her example. It took me a lot of years to implement leaving love notes around, however. Doesn't it seem like we're always too busy? Isn't it too much effort to jot down *I love you* and stick it in a school lunch box? Aren't we too preoccupied to write *Thanks for being you* and posting it on the bathroom mirror for our spouse to find? Guess what? It takes almost no time to be thoughtful. It only takes a bit of our focused attention when we have a pen in hand.

PURPOSE: *Opening our hearts helps us realize how much we have to be grateful for. When we train our minds to focus on love rather than on problems, we feel better.*

Rise and Fall

TRIGGER: When you get angry or have been faced with an angry person.

TOOL: Inhale, and as you do so, bring your shoulders up high (as if you're trying to touch your ears), then exhale slowly through your mouth, dropping and relaxing your shoulders. Shake your arms and say, "I release this energy."

We were due to depart for the airport in thirty minutes. My husband and my three children and I were headed to Virginia to visit my mother and stepfather. We hadn't been to their house for many years.

Suddenly I heard an earsplitting yell from my seventeen-year-old daughter: "WHERE ARE MY JEAN SHORTS?" She was downstairs in the laundry room making a ruckus. Next, I heard her stomping up the stairs. "MOM, YOU LOST MY SHORTS!" Although logic wasn't particularly helpful, I still felt compelled to reply that I had not lost her shorts, in fact had never even seen her shorts.

Sometimes, I have noticed, adolescents just completely melt down (okay, adults do too from time to time). This was one of those occasions. As if it was the straw that broke her back, my daughter-on-the-cusp-of-adulthood went in her room sobbing like a five-year-old. "I WON'T LEAVE THIS HOUSE UNTIL I FIND MY SHORTS!"

I followed her into her room to face a barrage of incoherent threats, tear-streaked screams, and general mayhem. I caught the angry fever and responded, "Oh yes you will!" Then I upped the ante: "You are going on this trip and that's final. We leave in twenty minutes!"

With my heart racing, I went downstairs, aware that adrenaline was coursing through my body. My serenity was out the window. I lifted my shoulders with a deep inhale and then dropped my shoulders, over and over again, watching my tension begin to dissipate. It became clear that what I needed to do was observe rather than absorb her energy.

I returned to her room and told her that I was truly sorry that she wasn't able to find her shorts. In a nonresistant manner, I said that in fact, she didn't have to go with us on this trip. However, she was going to need to call her grandmother and explain that she wasn't able to come because she couldn't find her . . . *shorts*. At this point, she couldn't help but offer a feeble smile.

Defeated, my daughter began putting her things in her suitcase. It took her a while to come out of the fit, so much so that the security guard at the airport said to her, "Guess you're having a bad day, huh?"

Me? Well, my day was going much better after I disengaged from anger.

PURPOSE: *When we engage angry energy, we lose our ability to think clearly. We begin to participate in an escalating cycle of resis-*

tance, reactivity, and even violence. However, when we stop the cycle by pausing and consciously releasing our attachment to the negativity, we develop a new healthy habit and begin to reclaim our center of inner peace.

TRIGGER: When your buttons get pushed and you're upset, maybe even on the verge of tears.

TOOL: Excuse yourself, get out of the situation, find the nearest water fountain, sink, or bottle of water and splash your face with cold water. If possible, get a wet washcloth or paper towel and hold it to the back of your neck or on your face until you cool off. Imagine your emotional fire being doused.

Married for sixteen years, my husband and I were going through a divorce. Like most people, I hadn't expected to get divorced after saying "I do" at the age of twenty-five. But like many millions of people, I found myself going through a divorce nonetheless.

Everyone warned me that "war" was inevitable. Divorced friends advised me to hire a bulldog lawyer to protect myself. Other friends warned my soon-to-be ex that I would try to take him to the cleaners. I think we both knew that such behaviors would not only be demeaning to ourselves but would be damaging to our three children. And so I hired a collaborative attorney and worked very intentionally to keep the process amicable.

But that's not to say that buttons never got pushed . . .

One extremely hot summer day, sitting alone in my part-time separation apartment, I had a phone conversation with my soon-to-be ex-husband about, oh, light things—like child custody, finances, broken hearts. Things were said, low blows were dealt, emotions were rising. In retrospect, I can hardly recall the specifics. I just know that he said something to upset me, and I said something back to upset him, and so on and so on . . .

Meanwhile, I began to get extremely hot, literally burning up. I told him that I didn't think we could talk productively anymore and that we should try again later. He agreed and we hung up. It was *so* hot. I started to feel a little faint. I started to cry. I started to feel more faint.

I have a relatively rare condition called anhidrosis, which is the inability to sweat. I know it sounds strange, and the only other person I know who suffers from it is my sister, but it means that we cannot cool our bodies down in a normal manner. So when we get hot, it's a real problem! Personally, the only thing I've found to cool me down and avoid heat exhaustion is to find cool water, a lot of it, and quickly.

So I went to the bathroom and began to splash cool water on my face. Then I soaked a washcloth in the water, wrung it out, and held it over my face until I started to chill. And that's when I noticed that not only was the cold water bringing my temperature down, it was bringing my upset down too. I felt calmer, comforted. I had a flash of association of my mother putting a cool compress on my forehead when I was sick with a fever. Somehow the cool cloth signaled to me that all would be well and this too would pass.

PURPOSE: *When we get overly stimulated in an emotional conversation, it's easy to allow our feelings to run away with us. As we get upset, we get physically and psychologically "flushed." A brief respite from our heated conversation allows us to gain awareness of our emotions, redirect our thinking, and calm our physical stress response. Using cool water as a means to bring relief to the body also brings relief to the mind and spirit. Let the cool healing waters remind you that peace is possible, even in the midst of a storm.*

RIGHT TURN

TRIGGER: When you are faced with hostile, attacking energy.

TOOL: See a mental YIELD sign. Take a deep breath and exhale slowly. Be silent and still. As you release your resistance, say, "I agree with you," or if that isn't possible to say, then try, "I can see how you would think that."

It was a beautiful late spring afternoon, the kind of warmish day in New England that feels like heaven on earth after a long hunkered-down winter. The palest green shoots were bursting forth on the trees. I felt intoxicated by nature's rebirth.

So there I was in my car, filled with spring's optimism and toting a grocery list. I entered the parking lot and started to turn toward a spot . . . no wait, I saw a closer one in the next row and veered toward it . . . nah, I turned again, going out farther, deciding to take the opportunity to walk.

Honk! There was a chestnut-haired middle-aged woman shooting me the finger. Okay, maybe I was driving a little indecisively. Maybe I deserved that. Or maybe that lady was having a really bad day.

So I went into the grocery store, minding my own business, and somewhere between the bananas and the broccoli, this woman came up to me with rage on her face and began berating me for my "crazy" driving and how she ought to call the cops, that I should have a ticket for such reckless behavior, and how I might have killed somebody.

I have to say that I had *never* been chastised in public by a complete stranger (or even by a friend, for that matter). I felt my heart start to race as adrenaline flushed through my body. I looked around to see if anyone might come to my aid. No one. How could the produce section be so empty?

I felt the urge to defend myself and counterattack. Aggressive responses lingered on the tip of my tongue: *You bitch. How dare you? What is your problem? Who do you think you are?* How easy it would be to match her aggression with my own aggression, allowing the altercation to escalate.

But something was different for me that day. It was the day I learned the power of nonaggression. I found myself saying simply, "You're right. I should be more cautious when I'm driving."

Silence.

She looked stunned. The energy deflated out of her like a balloon releasing air. She stood there for a moment not knowing what to do. "Yeah . . . Yeah . . . well, watch it," she finally stammered. With a look of confusion, she turned and walked away. Spring was back in the air.

PURPOSE: *When we react to aggressive energy with more aggressive energy, the cycle can only escalate. Angry people are often hurt, afraid, worried, or desperate to be heard. Their aggression toward us is a response to their perceived aggression on our part. However, if we take the bait, we just get caught in the vicious cycle. When we offer agreement or understanding instead of defensiveness, their aggressive energy dissipates and we remain free. The peaceful response for everyone is to disengage.*

TRIGGER: When you're feeling greedy, stuck, stubborn, or selfish.

TOOL: Let your shoulders relax, and breathe in while you say to yourself, "In giving, I receive." Breathe out slowly and say, "In receiving, I give."

"May I have an opening bid? Ten dollars?" The auctioneer scanned the audience and noted as I raised my paper paddle, which displayed my bidder number. "We have a bid, now twenty dollars, who will bid twenty dollars?" A silver-haired woman with a beaming smile across the room—a woman who happened to be an acquaintance of mine—raised her paddle.

We were at a community fund-raiser auction. The object in question was a stunning hand-thrown ceramic-lidded vase valued at one hundred dollars. Many of the items in this auction were going for peanuts, with the auctioneer begging us to bid. This item, however, had attracted the attention of both me and my friend.

The auctioneer, relishing this minor bidding war, proclaimed, "*Eighty* dollars . . . we have *eighty* dollars . . . do I hear *one hundred*?" No, this item had gone out of my range and I backed down. I smiled reluctantly and admitted defeat. "SOLD! To the silver-haired lady."

After the auction, I approached my comrade and said, "Con-

gratulations on winning that vase. It is quite unique and beautiful." She turned to look me in the eye, and with a gentle grin, she
said, "I would like you to have it. It's my gift to you." I stammered
and sputtered as she placed the coveted object in my hand.

"What? . . . Uh . . . I couldn't possibly."

"Then consider it your gift to me, to receive it."

I was dumbfounded. Such an act of selfless generosity left me
speechless. I wondered if I would ever be able to follow her example of graciousness.

About one year later, I was on a New Hampshire beach comb-
ing the sands with my husband for sea glass (a favorite pursuit).
Daniel is a master at spotting these gems from the sea. As it turned
out, he found a very rare white piece that was in the perfect shape
of a heart. I couldn't believe its beauty.

As we strolled along, I ran into two friends whom I hadn't seen
in a while. We chatted about a mutual friend, commented on the
gorgeous late summer weather, and then they asked what we were
looking for (it is a strange sea-glass-collecting conundrum to be
looking down at the ground for the glass rather than looking out
at the stunning seascape). I showed them my handful of beach
treasures.

One of the women exclaimed, "Oh, look at that one! It's a perfect heart shape. I collect heart-shaped rocks from all over the
world."

Suddenly, remembering a gift to me, I felt the spirit move me
to offer this gift to *her*. "Why don't you take it," I suggested.

She responded, "Huh? . . . No, no."

"I'd like you to have it as my gift to you . . . and your gift to me is to receive it," I answered.

There, I did it. And it wasn't so hard, after all. In fact, what I realized is that in giving, you receive just as in receiving, you give. Buddhists believe that attachment is nothing more than a source of eventual suffering. Generosity is like discovering the keys to the door of a self-made prison.

PURPOSE: *Sometimes when we feel the most needy and greedy, that is the perfect time to give a little something (attention, agreement, time, presence). The act of giving opens our hearts and softens our resistance to others. Generosity is a tonic to relationships, like a shower of joy. Likewise, receiving with grace is a gift to the giver. Using this tool reminds us of this win-win exchange of goodwill energy.*

Rag Doll

TRIGGER: When you have a stressful evening with your children.

TOOL: Intentionally take a break: Go into a room by yourself, lean over like a rag doll, and touch your toes. Stay like this for a few moments and then crouch down to the ground with your head bent over your body as if you're about to do a somersault. Letting your body relax, imagine that you are watching this evening from the vantage point of heaven. Note how precious every detail is in light of the fact that all of it will completely cease to exist in but a few years.

When my children were five, three, and one, I was completely consumed with mothering. With one in diapers, one in preschool, and one in kindergarten, I was immersed in major labor-intensive mom duty twenty-four/seven. And I loved it. Those days seemed long and spacious.

One evening at a community event, I ran into a friend whose only son had just left for college. She saw me with my brood, and as she stared long and hard at the eager little faces around my legs, she said, "It goes so quickly. Enjoy every day because one day soon, before you can even imagine it, they'll be leaving home."

"I know," I quipped. "I will." But the truth is that I absolutely couldn't imagine it. On some bizarre level, I felt like it wouldn't happen. Everyone said that the years went by quickly, but it seemed to me that the days went by so slowly. These darlings surely would be my babies forever. Being so close to the minutiae of daily living, I couldn't see how they were changing and growing, literally every day. Their childhood seemed endless to me.

But of course, they did grow up and now they're leaving home one after the other, just as my friend forecast.

When I was in high school, I played the part of Mrs. Webb in the famous Thornton Wilder play *Our Town*. In it, the character of Emily dies during childbirth. During the third act she has an opportunity to relive one day in her life. She picks her twelfth birthday. As she returns to earth, she notices everyone living their life by rote, glazed to the miracles around them. She is heartbroken with the realization that humans don't cherish life while they have it.

Don't we all have a tendency to go through ordinary days without relishing our time? Don't we rush through our evening routines, from activity to dinner to homework to bedtime, dropping into bed exhausted? Do we ever actually stop to appreciate life while we're living it instead of only remembering it wistfully once it's gone?

Whether children grow up or whether life ceases altogether, one thing is for certain: Nothing lasts forever. The life you're currently living will change beyond recognition in less time than you think. So notice it now as a slice of impermanent pie. Savor the wonder of every morsel . . . and then release when it's time to let go.

PURPOSE: *When we momentarily stop the stressful whirlwind with a "pattern interrupt," we gain a fresh perspective. We're able to create the necessary distance to see our circumstances with new eyes. This tool helps us wake up, to actually realize the richness of our lives while we're living them. "Enjoy, savor, and release" is a recipe for inner peace.*

TRIGGER: **When someone either compliments you or criticizes you.**

TOOL: **After you hear or read a compliment or criticism, and you are alone, hold your hands in front of you, palms facing the ceiling. Holding a good opinion in one hand and a bad opinion in the other, balance them like a scale. Hold one side down low, as if it had weight, and then let the weight fall off and balance it back to equal. Hold the other side down low, as if it had weight, and then balance it back to equal. Say, "I am more than their opinion."**

I once attended a lecture on spirituality, and the extremely articulate speaker told his audience that there were three important things that we were *not*. He explained:

1. You are *not* what you do—the roles that you play in this world or your work.
2. You are *not* what you own—the stuff that you accumulate, the fanciest gadgets.
3. You are *not* what people say about you, either positive or negative.

The lecture was a revelation because so many of us behave as if our entire identity is based exactly on these three things: what we do, what we own, and what people say about us.

I think back on the third point frequently because I have chosen work that gives people many opportunities to either compliment or criticize me. With my writing, I am open to the opinions of readers who can post either favorable or unfavorable words about my work on reader reviews. With my public speaking, especially at professional workshops, I usually receive evaluation forms where I am meticulously judged and measured.

I know that if I allowed myself to become elated when someone "likes" me or crushed if someone doesn't, I would be doomed to a weightless self-esteem. Instead, when I remain internally anchored and understand that outside comments do not have the power to make me whole or make me empty, then I am able to walk on solid ground.

I and I alone have the power to balance the scales. That is, my thoughts have the power to balance the scales. I can hear a criticism and think, *They're right; I'm no good,* or I can think, *I am more than their opinion.* At the same time, I must be wary of allowing praise to become the foundation for my identity. Treating both negative and positive opinions with equanimity (even-mindedness) offers enormous freedom.

PURPOSE: *When we cultivate equanimity, we find that we become more deeply anchored to our inner self. We become less vulnerable to other people's opinions. Otherwise, we are like a leaf blowing in the wind, whimsically tossed by one changing opinion after another. This tool develops inner strength, which results in inner peace.*

CHEESECLOTH

TRIGGER: Whenever you're in a crowded, loud environment or when you're being faced with a hostile encounter.

TOOL: Breathe in deeply and imagine yourself becoming a porous fabric, like a net or mesh, and let the fluid world— all sights and sounds—pass through you. Breathe out slowly and observe words, insults, glances, and emotions float through and around you while you remain unattached and nonreactive.

A few years ago, I was at an amusement park in Tennessee with my mother, sister, and five children between us. It was a gorgeous sunny summer day, and not surprisingly, the park was full to capacity. While the grounds were beautiful and well maintained, there were crowds of people *everywhere*.

There were lines of people out of the restaurants . . . lines of people at every ride . . . lines of people in front of concession carts . . . even lines of people outside the souvenir shops. I found myself starting to get a little agitated. Ever since I left New York City (where I lived for eleven years), I've been line phobic. I used to stand in crowded lines every day—on subway platforms, at the coffee shop, and in stores. I literally maxed out on my lifetime supply of patience for standing in lines.

So there we were, the eight of us in a long unshaded line for the kiddie roller coaster, and I closed my eyes and stood stock-still. My mother asked me, "Are you okay?" I answered, "Fine . . . I'm just building a shield around myself to block out the noise and stimulation." With that, I proceeded to imagine a castle wall around me. When I was done, my mother asked if it had helped. "I can't really tell," I said. "It took so much effort that now I'm even more exhausted."

Well, we managed to get through the lines, through the day, and everyone went back to the hotel with sticky cotton-candy smiles. Later, telling my best friend about the day at the amusement park (she too suffers from a mild case of sensory integration syndrome), she said, "You're not supposed to put a shield around you—that has resistant energy in it, too much blocking. You're supposed to let all the energy pass *through* you, like you're cheesecloth."

What the heck is cheesecloth? I thought.

I'm not sure I've ever seen cheesecloth, but I got the idea. Mesh. Transparency. Let the noise, lights, chaos flow through and beyond me. I use this all the time now and I can attest that the accepting cheesecloth technique is more effective than the resistant shield technique. And if I'm really in a place of surrender, as all the stimulation passes through me, I start to relax and merge with all the action. After all, we're all connected.

PURPOSE: *When we accept stimulation or negative energy without resistance, we break down the barriers between self and other. The energy moves through and past us without sticking to us. Watching that energy wash over us without consequence trains our brains to be nonreactive and lets us move into a place of peace.*

Sensory Spotlight
Shortcuts to Weave Mindfully

When I was forty-six years old, I had the amazing good fortune to get remarried to a wonderful man. And not only that, but our honeymoon was a trip of a lifetime to Bali (talk about the middle-aged woman's dream come true!). We found ourselves madly in love in a tropical wonderland.

We also found ourselves . . . smoking cigarettes. Yes, I know, this is a dangerous habit with serious potential health repercussions, so I'm not condoning it. However, somehow, steeped in the decadent leisure of Southeast Asia, we found a midafternoon smoke entrancing and delicious. The Indonesians make clove cigarettes in actual flavors—such as mocha, espresso, and cappuccino. We're talking the Starbucks of cigarettes!

What clinched it for us was that smoking was not only accepted—it was ubiquitous. People smoked in restaurants,

bars, and all public places. I found a sugar-tipped clove ciga-
rette that was delightful. I think part of the allure was that it
satisfied each of my five senses: The sugar tip was sweet and
yummy, the aroma of cloves was intoxicating, the feel between
my fingers was delicate and smooth, the crackling of cloves
and tobacco was like a distant campfire, and the visual delight
of glowing embers and dancing smoke mesmerized me.

It felt leisurely . . . relaxing . . . peaceful. Having a smoke
was like a built-in break or respite from my busy mind. So I
can totally understand how the addiction begins. Fortunately,
our new habit did not travel back to the States with us, or I'd
be one of those people for whom taking a smoke break means
huddling outside in the New England winter.

Instead, my take-home lesson from my brief sojourn as a
smoker was an understanding of the power of the senses as
a portal to inner peace. We have our senses under our noses
(so to speak) but somehow neglect to notice.

Opportunities to treat ourselves with sights, sounds, tastes,
smells, and textures abound. These indulgences are easy and
everywhere. We just have to stop long enough to pay attention.
And when we pay attention regularly, we build and strengthen
new neural pathways in our brains so that after a while, this
peace-inducing habit begins to feel natural.

The ten Shortcuts in this section (two for each of the five
senses) are all about mindfulness. Mindfulness is a powerful
practice of being completely in the moment, nonjudgmentally
aware of everything happening. It means being alert and

present—amazingly, our senses are uniquely intent on helping us be in this state.

In the simple act of spotlighting a sense, the body is engaged, the mind is quieted, and the spirit is enhanced. So enjoy and let your senses guide you to a celebration of being alive; let them open a door to a deeper feeling of inner peace.

TOUCH TANK

TRIGGER: **When you feel tense or overwhelmed.**

PROP: Use a small box or basket in which to collect objects from nature as you come across them. You might include shells, sea glass, rocks, smooth stones, acorn caps, sticks, chestnuts, or pinecones. This is your "touch tank."

TOOL: Take a few moments to finger each object. Observe the details, one object at a time. Feel the texture in your hands. Brush an object to your cheek. Consider its origins and the conditions which brought it into being.

When I moved to the coast of New Hampshire in 1997, I was amazed to be living so close to the ocean. Every time I drove to the beach (a three-minute drive), it felt like a small miracle. I had never lived near the ocean and I could barely believe my good fortune. Although I'm more of a shade lover than a beach bum, I was comforted to know that the surf was nearby.

One of the perks of my new locale was a museum called the Seacoast Science Center at Odiorne Point State Park. This rich educational resource offers interactive exhibits, walking trails, summer camps, lecture series, and a cherished tidal pool touch tank. When my three children were preschool age, they used to love to go to the science center to finger the ocean treasures in this huge forty-foot tank.

Dipping their hands into the salty water, they could walk their fingers amid mussels and clams, periwinkles and urchins, sea anemones and barnacles. But the best treasure of all was to touch a starfish nested in the seaweed. My children would squeal with delight and hold them up in the light—whereupon kindly employees would gently request that the starfish be kept safely *in* the water.

They remained fascinated for hours stroking lichens, sneaking up on hermit crabs, and scooping up sea slugs. The children left, only reluctantly, with pruny fingers and the animated question: "Mom, can we get a pet starfish?"

I'm also reminded of a unique restaurant experience I once had while on a vacation. We had sat down at our table, and amid the cutlery and napkins, there were three river rocks placed carefully at each place setting. When the waiter came to take our drink order, I asked, "What are these rocks?" He smiled with a twinkle in his eye and said, "We believe that dining should be a multisensory experience. We wanted to include touch." We did, in fact, spend the evening happily touching the stones.

Whether from the ocean or from the land, gather some natural treasures and enjoy their tactile pleasures.

PURPOSE: *When we experience the sensory delight of touching natural objects, we ground ourselves in the Now and redirect our worrisome, tired thoughts. Connecting to the details of nature opens our minds and hearts to the larger world beyond ourselves of which we are a part.*

LEND A HAND

TRIGGER: When you're feeling anxious or stressed.

TOOL: Place one hand on your upper chest between your collar bones and your other hand on your belly. Apply some light pressure, breathe deeply into your belly, and then as you exhale slowly, rub your hand in a circle on your upper chest.

One of my favorite experiences in college was singing with an a capella group. Ten women met several times a week for rehearsals, learning intricate harmonies, and sharing songs at parties, concerts, and jamborees. It was a blast!

During my senior year, we took a road trip from Massachusetts to California (actually we flew, but it was a road trip to us). We sang for community groups, in shopping malls, and in nursing homes. We even cut an album in a recording studio, and I had the solo in the song "California Dreamin'."

I was so excited! I got to put on headphones and sing into a microphone just like in the movies. The only problem? I was terrified. As we sang the song, my body began to shake. I was okay until I got to the actual "California dreamin'" line. Oops. Every time I hit the note on "Ca," my voice cracked.

So we tried it again. Just approaching the note caused my heart to race and my palms to tingle. "Ca"—again, my voice cracked. What was going on? This had never happened to me before, not in rehearsal and not in a performance. I started to get dizzy and my friends led me over to a couch in the studio where I could lie down.

Though I didn't know about panic attacks at the time, I realize now that that's exactly what I was experiencing. I didn't know what to do . . . I started to tear up, unable to get a good breath. And then, one of my fellow singers said, "Whenever I got upset when I was a little girl, my mother would put her hand on the top of my chest and breathe with me."

And with that, my friend laid her hand across the top of my sternum, pressed lightly, and breathed. She rubbed in a gentle circle and told me to close my eyes and imagine a safe place. What I imagined was my mother making this gesture to me as a scared child. I found the image so dear, so maternal and caring, that I began to relax. My friend said, "Just put your hand there," and she guided my own hand to rest on my collarbone. "It will calm you down."

Ah, the power of my own touch and the slowing rhythm of my breath. After about five minutes, I had relaxed enough to try again. Feeling supported by my friends, I kept my hand on my chest throughout the song . . . and guess what? I sang it perfectly.

PURPOSE: *When we exhale deeply, our body responds by calming itself. The laying on of hands has long been considered a healing art. Reiki and massage are modern-day variations of an ancient tradition. We have the power to offer gentle comfort to ourselves through the power of touch. And in the self-soothing comfort of this tool, we encounter peace.*

ALMOND JOY

TRIGGER: **When you have a snack.**

PROP: **A handful of small snack food (nuts, M&Ms, raisins, popcorn, etc.).**

TOOL: Line up your small snacks like a train in front of you. Focus on this task and then eat one piece at a time, chewing and swallowing completely before you eat the next piece. Eat at least three pieces this way, focusing on the texture, the taste, and the experience.

I used to never notice what I ate—I mean *really* notice. And I ate all day long. There was breakfast, lunch, dinner, and I usually slid in a midmorning snack, an afternoon snack, and a pre-bedtime snack. (I'm hypoglycemic, okay?) And yet, even though I encountered food every few hours or so, I rarely paid attention.

There are those who live to eat and those who eat to live, and for better or for worse, I seemed to be in the latter category. Once I was in a restaurant, and the waitress came over midway through my lunch to apologize that she had mistakenly brought me a chicken salad sandwich when I had ordered a tuna sandwich. I was halfway through my sandwich already and I hadn't even noticed the mistake!

Were my taste buds dulled? Maybe. But more likely, I think I didn't notice my food because I was always noticing everything else. If I was dining with family or friends, I focused on our conversations. If I was eating alone in a restaurant, I typically noticed the people and sounds around me. When I ate alone at home, I often read or got lost in my daily preoccupations. I almost never stopped just to focus on the food that nourished me.

I took an online course about attention when my own inattention really hit home. One of the daily exercises was to spend the day mindfully noticing my food. I thought this was a great idea but I kept forgetting! I forgot all day long. In fact, that particular day I was in such a rush, I gulped down food particularly mindlessly. I might as well have been eating mush.

I was so embarrassed by my utter failure at this exercise that the next day, I wrote notes to myself to remember to eat mindfully. And so, indeed, I spent the first few moments of each meal forcing myself to stop and attend to the taste and texture of my food. I realized that food is a minor miracle . . . and we get to experience it multiple times a day!

What a multisensual delight: the aromas, the flavors, the textures, and crunches. All this wonder *and* it keeps our bodies functioning. So have a bit of fun with this tool and put your attention on each and every bite.

PURPOSE: *When we slow down and spend a moment in quiet awareness, when we take our attention off of our worries and instead pay attention to our sense of taste, we get a break from the relentless chatter in our minds and experience gratitude.*

TRIGGER: When you are eating.

TOOL: Look at your food and ask yourself, "Where did this food come from?" (Cheese from Vermont? Almonds from California? Grapes from Chile? A factory in North Dakota? A farm in Wisconsin?) Imagine the environment that created this item that you're enjoying and imagine all the parts in the journey that brought it to your table.

Several years ago, I had the thrilling opportunity to visit China. When we entered the immense airport in Beijing, I started to feel a bit woozy. We had been traveling for more than eighteen hours, and I hadn't eaten or slept as much as I would have liked. My husband and I were in a long customs line when I started to feel dizzy, weak, and nervous. At first, I passed it off as jet lag, but then the symptoms got worse.

I began to tremble, to slur my speech, to lose my vision. I wondered if I was having a panic attack or worse . . . a stroke? My husband held me up and force-fed me a granola bar. He suspected that I was having a low-blood-sugar attack, and in fact, I was. Within several minutes of eating, I started to feel better.

After that trip, we confirmed that I suffered from hypoglycemia. Since then, I've learned a lot about how the brain reacts when it is deprived of sufficient glucose and more than I care to know about the glycemic index. I've also learned how to keep my blood sugar fairly stable by avoiding processed sugar and white carbs, in addition to eating every couple of hours. As a result, my relationship to food has changed. I've come to fairly worship each and every morsel as my lifeline to consciousness and good health.

One day I was sitting at my kitchen table paying homage to a rye cracker with goat cheese and some cashews. I casually glanced at the tin of nuts to discover that the cashews were from Brazil. Intrigued, I looked at the package of goat cheese: from France. The rye crackers? Imported from Finland! It was like the United Nations in my kitchen.

My world began to expand as I noticed my kiwis from New Zealand, my olive oil from Italy, my wine from upstate New York, and my chai tea blended with leaves from India. And for each item, I knew there were hundreds of people involved in the growing, processing, packaging, transporting, moving, and stocking to get it on a shelf in my neighborhood where I purchased it and brought it home.

I felt so connected to the chain of industry, to the circle of life! Now it seems I can hardly eat a bite without investigating where my food comes from and imagining its exciting journey from its origins to my mouth.

PURPOSE: *When we cultivate a vision of a broader connectedness, we blast out of the confines of our own small worlds. Seeing our food*

CRYSTAL FLAME

TRIGGER: When you are stressed and need a break.

PROP: A candle.

TOOL: Light a candle and look into the flame for a minute. Notice the colors and the changing shape. Can you see the hot air as it rises? Gaze at the flame as if you are staring into a crystal ball. Let the light mesmerize and calm you. When you blow out the candle, watch the smoke rise until it completely dissipates.

My husband and I were on a vacation in the Berkshire Mountains of Massachusetts over New Year's Eve. We stayed in a beautiful historic inn that advertised a "gourmet candlelit breakfast." Wow! I had heard of romantic candlelit dinners but never a candlelit *breakfast*. I was intrigued.

In the chill of the winter morning, even without the darkness of night, I found the single point of light fascinating. I could hardly keep my eyes off the flickering flame. Its meditative properties drew me in, inducing a calm and relaxed state.

I had recently, in fact, rediscovered the serene properties of candlelight at night just the month before when a hurricane-like storm with winds gusting seventy miles per hour had left us without power for nearly three days. During that time, we huddled around firelight and candlelight with nothing else to distract us.

Life unplugged with no television, no Internet, no movies—nothing but candlelight and conversation—felt like a gift. When the electricity returned—okay yes, I was overjoyed to have hot water and heat—but I was a little reluctant to embrace the garish shock of electric lighting. I had learned that candlelight, in the night *and* in the day, mesmerized.

There is a reason why candlelight is so often used to grace special, celebratory events—it's hypnotic, comforting, beautiful. So, when you're feeling stressed, light a flame and simply enjoy it, rest in it. I keep a candle in almost every room of my house now. I've become something of a candle queen. I find their presence soothing and reminiscent of slower times. Allow yourself, for a moment, to be entranced.

PURPOSE: *When we slow down and redirect our minds to an awareness of simple color, light, and movement, we connect to the sacred flame within us.*

DOUBLE TAKE

TRIGGER: When you're feeling bored or restless.

TOOL: Sit down and observe an object intently for several moments. Start to notice things that you hadn't noticed before. Follow every inch . . . every corner . . . notice how the light lands on the object . . . witness the minute details. Try to see the object in a new way.

I was writing at my computer on a rainy Saturday afternoon. The kids were watching a movie in the family room when, all of a sudden, I heard a loud and booming *crash*. My heart skipped a beat.

The kids started yelling, "Mom, a picture fell off the wall."

"Which picture?" I said.

"The one with the little bird in the corner," my daughter answered.

Huh? I wondered. I didn't remember any picture with a bird in a corner. So I walked into the room to discover my favorite painting over the fireplace had become the victim of gravity and a weak nail. I studied the painting with its stunning sunset over a lake. "What bird?" I asked.

"Look in the corner," said my daughter. "See the little bird?"

Wow. Lo and behold, there was a small bird in the corner. I had been so preoccupied with looking at the sunset and the lake that I had never even looked in the corner. In fact, I wondered whether I had ever really *looked* at this painting in all its rich detail.

This reminded me of an attention exercise I once participated in during a writing workshop in which we were advised to hold an object, look at it, and write down twenty descriptive details. Just when I thought I had noted every possible detail, I would stare at the object, and almost as if by magic, I would notice something new.

How many of us actually *look* at the objects around us? Do we ever stop long enough to see them? Do we ever stop even longer to let the fine details emerge and come into focus?

It's a great irony that we often spend a lot of time, energy, effort, and money to acquire "stuff," and yet in the end we rarely take the time to really absorb and admire any of it. Let this tool be your permission to linger over the fine details.

PURPOSE: *When we take a moment to absorb the intricate details of an object, we stop the stream of thought that normally occupies our minds. We also bring fresh perspective to our sight, which can translate back into our lives. Finally, we get to experience the refreshment of savoring the details of an object. This is an antidote to our usual experience of going about life without really "seeing" anything.*

STOP 'N' SMELL

TRIGGER: **Before you begin cooking dinner.**

PROP: **A fragrant item in the kitchen. Four good standbys are (1) ground coffee or coffee beans, (2) a jar of peanut butter, (3) vanilla extract, or (4) rosemary.**

TOOL: **Choose a fragrance that triggers positive emotions for you. Close your eyes, take a big sniff, linger for several moments, and let the experience of the aroma fill you.**

When I was a little girl, we had hyacinths that bloomed every year. They came up on the side of the house near the driveway. I used to bury my nose in them, inhaling their powerful perfume. Every year I would look forward to early spring when they made their annual appearance.

Even now I eagerly anticipate their spring arrival. Although I no longer have any growing beside my house, I always make it a point to find some hyacinths to smell. I've actually been known to walk on a stranger's property to smell their hyacinths!

The curious thing to me is that even after forty years, the smell of hyacinths instantly transports me to the early 1970s beside a brick house in Dallas, Texas. Amazing! As if by magic, smells can transport us through time.

Aromas soothe. They calm and entice us. If you've had a bad head cold, you know how flat and lifeless life seems when you can't smell. Without your olfactory nerves in top shape, you can't even taste. So find a place to stick your nose and breathe in deeply. Let yourself get carried away.

PURPOSE: *When we "take in," and really embrace a positive experience, it activates calming mechanisms in our bodies. Anchoring ourselves in the present moment of a delicious aroma, we not only give our sense of smell a well-deserved treat, but we also allow the incessant chatter in our minds an opportunity to be quiet.*

HAIR-RAISING

TRIGGER: **When you're washing your hair.**

TOOL: **Pour the shampoo in your hand and sniff the aroma.
Close your eyes and as you lather your hair, imagine yourself
in a wonderfully pleasant faraway place. Concentrate on the
fragrance and let the experience sink into your body and mind.**

One hot summer, I visited my mother at her home in Virginia. Over
breakfast, we discussed the plans for the day: a little sightseeing,
a little swimming, a little snoozing—perfect.

I went upstairs to shower, wash my hair, and dress for the day.
I had forgotten to bring my shampoo so I casually grabbed a
bottle that she had in her shower. Old Spice. *You've got to be kidding,* I thought. I didn't even know that they made a shampoo.
Didn't my grandfather wear Old Spice cologne?

And then it happened. As I smelled the dollop of shampoo
headed for my head, I was transported in time and place to my
grandfather's lap. It was the late 1960s in Arlington, Texas. I was
allowed to curl up beside him in his big easy chair while we
watched the Dallas Cowboys on the television. A TV tray beside
us was heaped with Cheetos and chocolate-chip cookies, a Dr
Pepper for me and a Budweiser for him.

During the commercials, he tickled me and I squealed with delight. He smelled of spice and the sea, a fragrance so distinct that I still associate it with him to this day. I loved that smell as I loved my grandfather.

Whoa—back in the shower in Virginia. I was amazed that a smell in a bottle could act as a time machine. I hadn't thought of my long deceased grandfather in quite a while, yet I felt as if we had just had a short visit. Could shampoo do all that?

When I returned to New Hampshire, I decided to capitalize on the soothing and transformative powers of shampoo. So I went shopping. Did I want the aromatic properties of white nectarine and pink coral flower? How about a trip to the tropics with fusion orchid and coconut milk? It's hard to choose between grapefruit and lemongrass or a concoction of French lavender with chamomile.

Aromatherapy has long been recognized as a potent way to balance and harmonize the body and mind, a natural way to enhance psychological well-being. Most of us don't realize that we have that healing opportunity each and every time we wash our hair!

PURPOSE: *Breathing in the heady fragrance of different shampoos has the dual effect of stimulating our sense of smell and also transporting us to another place. Taking the time to let a positive experience sink in helps to balance the store of negative memories in our brains and stimulates immediate calming effects in our bodies. Let your imagination match the smell and take you on a mini-vacation. You'll emerge from the shower peacefully restored and refreshed.*

TRIGGER: When you transition between daily events, such as before meals or before you start a project.

PROP: A bell, a singing bowl, a chime.

TOOL: Ring your bell, or sound your chime. As you do, close your eyes and listen to the sound. Breathe the ringing tones into your body. Feel the sound vibrations in the air. Listen even as the sound dissipates into the air and into stillness.

When I was a little girl, my family was active in a local Congregational church. We went every Sunday. I also attended the youth group, and we gathered for regular fellowship dinners. Most of all, I enjoyed the sense of community. But my favorite annual event was listening to the bell choir on Christmas Eve.

The men and women, clad in deep scarlet robes, assembled along the tables in front of the congregation. They donned their white gloves and, grasping the leather handles, readied their bells by flipping them quickly to their chests. Then the conductor waved his baton to signal the beginning of the song and one by one . . . then in pairs and trios . . . the musicians flicked their arms and wrists forward, releasing bell sound after magical bell sound. At the end of each song, they held their arms extended, letting the tones wash over the audience. It felt like we were dusted with magic.

One year, the youth choir was asked to participate. This was very exciting news! I was assigned the "A bell," and I was to ring it loudly on any occasion that an A note was included in a chord. I was nervous, but at fourteen years of age, I felt ready to take on the challenge of "Carol of the Bells."

There I stood between the G and the C bells. *Ding. Dong. Ding. Dong.* It was amazing! I almost felt like bells were ringing inside my body. I had never experienced anything like it . . . the resonance seemed to fill me. I was afloat with the exhilarating sensation of sound.

Ever since, I've had a soft spot for bells—from big cathedral bells to tiny jingle bells. Bell tones can elicit emotions from joy and merriment to a sober centeredness. Whatever the feeling, bells touch our hearts and souls.

PURPOSE: *When we create a pause in our day to focus on the healing vibrations created by sound, we experience peace through increased awareness, allowing our spirits to be touched.*

TRIGGER: When you're having trouble sleeping at night.

TOOL: Close your eyes and tune in to all the sounds around you. As you hear a sound, label it: *barking dog, airplane overhead, dishwasher running, cough, crickets outside, honking horn,* and so on. Listen more deeply. Do you hear the sound of your breath? Do you hear the beat of your own heart? Feel yourself relax into the experience. Count each exhalation.

I know the wee hours of the dark morning . . . a time familiar to night owls, nursing mothers, and insomniacs. Who knows why, but I have suffered my fair share of nights with insomnia.

I have tried resisting and railing against the thwarted sleep cycle (to no avail, I assure you). I have tried "making friends" with my sleeplessness, getting up to read and write. I have suffered through what I call "head clangers" (my own personal consequence of sleep deprivation). I have gotten trapped in insomniac cycles that last over a week before I can get my energy rebalanced. Every time it feels like a curse.

During one such a nocturnal awakening, I became consumed with listening to my dear husband's "heavy breathing" (aka snoring). My attention shifted from my own tormented condition to focusing on this particular sound, thinking to myself, *It's like a buzz saw, no, more like a bulldozer, no, that just sounded like a jackhammer.*

I nudged him over on his side at which point the nasal rumble ceased. And in that vacuum of sound, I suddenly started listening to the silence. I concentrated my attention and, to my surprise, I heard my clock ticking. I heard a car in the distance . . . a child's cough . . . a creak in the wall . . . a stray cat's meow . . . the wind at the window. I floated into the night symphony and then I noticed a new sound—the sound of my own breathing! As I cued into the melody of my breath, I counted each exhalation.

I discovered that losing myself in sounds relieved me from my mental preoccupations. Now when I find myself inadvertently burning the midnight oil, I close my eyes and listen to the humming and buzzing and shuffling and chirping. Then I listen to (and count) the music of my own breath . . . a lullaby that takes me, sooner or later, to dream land.

PURPOSE: *When we bring ourselves into the moment and redirect our minds from our troubles, we become aware of the music of life all around and within us. This activity calms our bodies and creates a disruption to the cycle of annoying thoughts that keep us awake.*

The Peace Portals

Chill Out!

Shortcuts to Calm Your Body

Stress takes a pretty deadly toll on the body. The list of diseases scientifically linked to stress seem endless: hypertension, heart disease, high blood pressure, ulcers, heart attacks—not to mention the ordinary knots in your stomach, aches in your back, sleepless nights, and general nervousness.

Our poor bodies! The blood, organs, tissues, and bones work diligently to keep us upright, yet stress launches us into one heart-pounding, artery-clogging reaction after another. What's a body to do but break down on occasion?

In 1975, Herbert Benson published his classic text, *The Relaxation Response*. It was a groundbreaking work at the time with specific instructions on how to "relax" the body in order to reduce stress. Basically it taught Westerners how to meditate without using Eastern lingo. Its primary breakthrough was recognizing the mind-body connection: a stressful mind wreaks havoc on the body, and likewise, relaxing the body helps to chill the mind.

When I was in high school, several years after that seminal work was published, I took a class on stress management and we were taught progressive relaxation as a means of stress reduction. The concept was to imagine an egg breaking on the top of your head and spreading warm liquid down your body, moving down your head, down your neck, over your shoulders, and down your arms scanning all the way down to your feet.

I liked the technique so much that I would gather small groups of friends in my bedroom and guide them through it, relaxing us all from the top of our heads to the tips of our toes. My friends loved the exercise and professed that learning this little ritual helped them get through the many pressures of high school!

The tools in this section are designed to reduce the stress in our bodies and/or wake us up. By stimulating the calming wing of our nervous system, we dampen our reaction to stress, lift our mood, reduce our blood pressure and relax our resistance to external circumstances. When we use them consistently, we actually train our bodies and minds to relax naturally in situations where we previously would have responded stressfully.

It's hard to relax the mind if your body is tied up in knots so these Shortcuts stretch you into a place where inner peace can flourish. Furthermore, when you focus on and ground yourself in the body, you begin to access the present moment (leaving behind the past and the future). Ruminating about problems backward or forward in time is merely a spin cycle for the mind and soul. Resting in the Now is always more peaceful.

Let your body be your anchor to inner peace.

TRIGGER: When putting a key in a lock (of your house, your office, your gym locker, your car).

TOOL: As you put in the key, imagine that you are unlocking the stress in your body. Let yourself pause for one slow, deep breath. Inhale deeply, extending your belly (as if you were trying to look pregnant), and then let air into your back and your chest. Hold briefly and exhale slowly, eventually squeezing the air out. Pull your belly button back to your spine to expel the air out of your abdomen. Go *very slowly*, putting your attention on the pause after inhalation and then the long, low exhale. One deep, low breath is "key" to stress management.

One of my lifelong hobbies is singing and performing. I have performed in children's choirs, adult choirs, community choruses, on musical theater stages, and in opera houses. I love to sing! When I lived in New York City for eleven years, I also took the opportunity to take some voice lessons. I don't think I ever seriously considered a career in singing—sopranos in New York are a dime a dozen—but still I wanted to understand the technique of singing.

One of my teachers—let's call her Alice—was a tall, dramatic woman whose home was a small, dark labyrinth of a place. Beside the piano was an enormous vase filled with peacock feathers. Turkish-looking fabrics were swathed around the windows. Candles and crystals lay on low wooden tables. I might have come for a séance as easily as a voice lesson.

I'm indebted to Alice because she taught me how to breathe—really breathe. One rainy afternoon she had me lie down on my back on her plush Oriental carpet with the instruction, "Watch your belly as you breathe." As it turns out, your belly expands *out* as you breathe *in*. Here I had always thought the opposite, that when you take a big breath, your stomach sucks in and your chest puffs out. That day, I experienced a full three-part breath with my belly out first . . . and then my back expanding into the floor . . . and then my chest rising last.

I've since used this three-part breath to calm panic attacks, to hit a high C, and to ride out birthing contractions (okay, yes, the epidural was actually more effective, but still . . .). Try this breath and see for yourself.

PURPOSE: *This deep exhale has an immediate calming effect on the body. Breathing low in your belly activates the parasympathetic nervous system, thus releasing feel-good endorphins. Your mind takes its cues from the body: tight body, tense mind . . . relaxed body, peaceful mind. The belly breath also expands the lungs which keeps them supple and flexible as we age. And finally, this kind of breathing brings extra oxygen to the brain, which just simply makes us feel better.*

TRIGGER: **When you are putting clean dishes away.**

TOOL: **As you stack the plates, put away the glasses, and fill the cutlery drawer, focus intently on the textures and sounds around you. Notice the clatter, the clink, the chiming sounds. Experiment with different ways of filling the cupboards—quietly, loudly, two hands on a dish, one hand on a dish, and so forth. Tap your fingers on the plate, on the cup. Let your thoughts float away as you put your fingers and attention on the minute details of this simple task.**

My mother held up a dish with a bold geometric pattern. "How do you like this design?" she asked. "Too modern," I responded. She picked up another with big splashy flowers on it and turned toward me. "No," I said, preempting her question. "Way too flowery."

We were on a mission: tirelessly searching for the perfect plates for my first apartment. I was twenty-one years old, a young adult taking my turn at "making it" in New York, New York. My mother had come to visit, to appraise how I had settled into my new abode.

She was distressed to learn that I had been eating off of paper plates for over a month. Most of my home furnishings had been discovered in flea markets and thrift stores, but I hadn't found a set of acceptable plates—nor did I want the hodgepodge feel of mis-matched pieces. My mother had graciously agreed to buy a set of dishes for me as a home-warming gift. And so we were on the hunt.

Finally, after visiting an assortment of kitchen, home-decorating, and department stores, I found a simple set of earth-toned crockery with a delicate white flower design. Who knows why, but this particular pattern just called to me.

I adored those dishes! For many years, I hand-washed them with obsessive care, almost as if they were a special symbol of my new home and my new life.

Years later, these beloved dishes were replaced by more exten-sive sets and fancier china. Hand washing gave way to an efficient dishwasher. And before I knew it, emptying the dishwasher was a drudgery, a chore to be quickly squeezed in between other tasks.

However, when I use this Shortcut, I am reminded of my youth-ful exuberance at owning a simple plate. I pause, stopping long enough to marvel at the implements that make my meals visually appealing. Then I broaden my attention to notice the beauty of a juice glass, the feel of a porcelain cup, the sound of a spoon clink-ing against a butter knife. And I find that I am comforted by the stillness and wonder of my expanding world.

PURPOSE: *When we focus our attention on simple sounds and tex-tures, our thoughts lose their grip. This exercise in mindfulness reduces stress, clears our minds, and creates a pause that resets our default setting to inner peace.*

PLAY IT AGAIN, SAM

TRIGGER: When you find yourself grumbling over an unpleasant household chore (folding laundry, emptying the dishwasher, collecting garbage, preparing a meal, cleaning up the dishes, cleaning bathrooms).

TOOL: Sing a specific song or play special music when you're engaged in that unwanted chore. Decide to let yourself have a positive experience and actually let it fill your body with good sensations.

When my oldest daughter was in second grade, I distinctly remember going to a school open house and casually chatting with a father of one of her friends. For some reason, the topic of music came up, and he described to me how much his daughter loved listening to the Beatles. I left the conversation with the shocking realization that my children had never even heard of the Beatles, much less listened to their music—not "Let It Be," not "Yellow Submarine," not "Come Together"—nothing.

Of course they had heard a wide variety of songs from *Barney and Friends* and *Sesame Street*—along with a smattering of classical music from my CD collection. My musical range suddenly seemed woefully narrow, so I went out and bought the newly compiled Beatles album, *1*. And I decided to borrow a technique from the children's playpen days: to have special toys that were *only* available in the playpen. So I began playing the Beatles *only* when we were all folding clothes together. The chore actually became something of a treat.

Fortunately, they were too young to protest and they really liked the Beatles. I nearly fainted when, after school, my children would ask if they could fold clothes! Now all teenagers, this situation is quite unimaginable, though I believe they still associate the Beatles with folding laundry.

Anyway, it's a healthy habit to crank up some tunes or belt out a favorite song when you feel stymied by chores around the house. Try a Christmas carol or a cheerful song that you know helps shift your thinking toward happiness. Don't worry about how you sound—just let the music fill you and uplift your spirits.

PURPOSE: *When we bring some cheer into an otherwise mundane task, we redirect to a positive experience. Soaking in our positive emotions counteracts depressed moods, relaxes the body, and reduces the production of stress hormones. Training our minds to attend to a brighter side when faced with a boring or unpleasant chore brings gratitude and acceptance into our day-to-day activities. And practiced consistently, our world begins to brighten.*

UNDER THE SEA

TRIGGER: When feeling overwhelmed or overstimulated.

TOOL: Sit in a chair and lean over to touch your toes. Let yourself flop over, like a rag doll, completely relaxed. If it's not comfortable to lean over, then simply let your head rest down, chin to chest. Close your eyes, let your shoulders relax, and imagine yourself suspended in the depths of the sea. Notice the water far above you, choppy, churned, and tempestuous, while you rest untroubled in the still, deep ocean.

When I was in college, as a special once-in-a-lifetime Christmas present, my grandmother took me, my mother, and my sister on a Caribbean cruise. Three generations out on the open seas. We were beside ourselves with excitement.

One of the happy memories I have of that trip was snorkeling for the first time in my life. I will never forget the feeling of awe when I saw the clear enchanted world just below the surface. There were colorful fish, amazing coral, and a thousand unnamed wonders of the sea. I was, you might say, star*fish* struck.

Having just finished my final exams, I remember thinking that nothing down here cares whether I got an A in history; no fish cares what my GPA is. As I observed this vast and intricate world, the real world seemed a million miles away. Everything below was quiet, perfectly in balance, moving to its own synchronized rhythms. I was mesmerized.

Now, when I get overwhelmed by too many kids, too many to-do items, too many sounds, too many stressors, I sit in a chair, curl down, and imagine myself buoyant in the deep sea. There, life is quiet and still with a depth that is ultimately untouched by the turbulent surface of daily living.

PURPOSE: *Thinking of a peaceful experience and letting it sink in will counteract stress and anxiety. Our imagination can bring us to that deeper place within that knows stillness and peace. We carry the capacity for calm within us all the time—the trick is to pause long enough to connect to the source.*

TAP DANCE

TRIGGER: When you lack the energy to continue with a task; when you are feeling sleepy in the late afternoon.

TOOL: Close your eyes and take a deep breath. Tap your fingers on your head and face. Use the pointer, middle, and ring fingers of your left and right hands. Starting with your forehead, move to your eyebrows, your eyelids, under your eyes, your cheekbones, your ears, your nose, under your nose, down your cheeks, your chin, down your neck, and above your collarbone. Be aware of the sensations as you lightly tap your entire face, hitting key acupressure points. Once you get to your collarbone, move your fingers back up your face to end with light tapping on the top of your head. For a little extra *umph,* add a scalp massage while saying, "Awake my sleeping self, awake!"

For several years, I cohosted a radio program in Portsmouth, New Hampshire, called *Heart to Heart with Ashley and Andy.* It was a weekly live broadcast with a guest and special topic of emotional/ spiritual interest. Many of the subjects were serious, but we always managed to create fun and playful energy as we engaged in our heart-to-heart discussions.

One week we brought on a hypnotherapist to teach us about

the "Emotional Freedom Technique" (or EFT). EFT is a popular approach to alternative healing, which is based on tapping acupressure points. The full sequence has been proven to eliminate phobias, bad habits, aches and pains, as well as negative thought patterns. The technique involves tapping various points on the head, body, and hands, along with specific affirmations to solve certain problems. We had a rather hilarious time using my cohost as a guinea pig and trying to make the process "visual" for our radio audience.

This Shortcut, inspired by EFT, is a little more freestyle. Personally, I like to think of it as having a little tap-dancing session on my face . . . a facial à la Fred Astaire. Let your fingers do the tapping and see what feels good to you. Over time you'll discover what really resonates—maybe you'll find that you just love applying extra pressure to your cheekbones or your temples. Think of it as a custom massage that you design for your own relaxation and invigoration.

As we stimulate acupressure points, we also bring a healthy blood supply to the surface of the skin. Closing our eyes has the added benefit of giving our eyes a rest while our touch sense takes the driver's seat for a few minutes.

PURPOSE: *The physical aspect of this tool gives us a little energy boost and also brings us into the present moment. When we redirect our minds from our busy thoughts to an awareness of our bodies, we create a brief pause from the stresses that can wear us down.*

BE A TREE

TRIGGER: When you feel physically stiff, groggy, resistant, or emotionally stuck.

TOOL: Stand up and reach your arms overhead, stretching high as if to touch the sky. Close your eyes and imagine yourself as a tree: imagine your body as a strong trunk, your arms as branches, and your fingers as leaves. Imagine roots extending through your feet into the earth. Let yourself sway in the wind. Then lower your arms and pull up energy from your roots as you bring your arms again overhead. Breathe in deeply and exhale slowly. Feel yourself grounded, rooted, and connected to the majesty of trees.

My eighteen-year-old daughter, on the verge of leaving for college, wanted nothing to do with her mother or life at home. Unless I was offering to buy her new clothes, time with mom was pretty much a bore. And so it was a surprise when Elizabeth said, "I ordered a movie for us all to watch this weekend."

"Really?" I asked cautiously. "What is it?"

"*My Neighbor Totoro*," she responded. "My friends said it's awesome."

Super. I had never heard of this movie, but I later discovered that it was a G-rated 1988 Japanese anime film directed by Hayao Miyazaki.

So there we sat, me, Dan, and three teenage girls, watching a movie geared toward preschoolers. And yet we were all mesmerized! The charming film follows the lives of two young girls in rural Japan, their father, and their ill mother. The sisters discover Totoro, a forest spirit, along with other wood sprites.

My favorite scene was when the youngest girl plants rows of acorns in celebration of her mother's imminent return from the hospital. Unfortunately, the acorns don't sprout, despite her efforts. One night, just as she is giving up, Totoro and his band of wondrous spirit friends appear and, raising their hands over the garden, will the acorns to sprout. They pull and pull the seedlings into saplings and finally into the tallest of trees.

What a magical scene. How easy it is to forget the true miracle of a tree born from a seed. We are surrounded by trees and yet we hardly give them a thought, a glance, until perhaps we see one fall or logged in the spirit of development.

Trees . . . our neighbors . . . our inspiration . . . are an abundant symbol of grounded strength and a beautiful example of graceful surrender to life's seasonal transitions. Be a tree!

PURPOSE: *Paying attention to the details of our bodies and slowly exhaling calms our stress response to the world around us. When we stretch and breathe deeply, we are energized. We extend our limbs to connect to a classic natural symbol of strength and transformation, and we pull energy up from our roots. We can embody the energy of life that is the tree.*

TRIGGER: When feeling anxious, worried, or generally stressed out.

TOOL: Begin by breathing evenly in and out. Feel your pulse, either on your wrist or on the side of your neck. Focus your attention on the sensations of pressure against your fingers. Feel life beating within you. Count your heartbeat to at least twenty.

In the years after *Transcending Loss* was published, I did a lot of public speaking on the topic of grief at national professional conferences. Sometimes I traveled by air, sometimes by car. But in 1999, something completely unexpected happened.

I had given a talk in western Massachusetts and I had just started the three-hour drive back to my home in New Hampshire. I was feeling tired but also satisfied that I had met so many kind people at the conference. I was listening to some choral music when out of the blue, my heart started racing. Then my left hand went numb. And my palms became cold and clammy.

Heaven help me, I thought. *Am I having a heart attack? A stroke?* I wondered. I pulled off at the first exit and went into a gas station bathroom (which was so filthy, by the way, it was a wonder I didn't have a heart attack from the shock of it). I looked at myself in the mirror, and with my heart still racing, I realized that I was having a full-blown panic attack.

I was no stranger to panic attacks, but I had never had one while driving. If you've never had one, it's hard to describe the severity of symptoms and degree of distress that they usually bring. I've since learned to basically ignore panic symptoms, not giving them any attention whatsoever (and as a result, they've largely disappeared). But back in 1999, what was a girl to do but panic *more.*

I quickly realized the extent of my predicament. I was nearly three hours from home, with three small children waiting, and no logistical way for my husband to come retrieve me. I *had* to get back in that car and get myself home. But all I could imagine was tucking into a fetal position in the backseat.

After about five minutes of resting in the car, when I realized that my heart rate was not going to calm down, I turned on the ignition and white-knuckled my way back on the highway. Instinctively, I reached my left hand up to my neck to feel my pulse. I think I wanted reassurance that I was still alive. Or maybe I just wanted to feel the primal beat of life that pulses through all living things. Whatever the reason, I did it, and the simple act kept me anchored to reality.

I did get home. And since then, I have used the "Take the Pulse" Shortcut many times to ground and calm myself.

PURPOSE: *Connecting to our heartbeats and stilling our bodies has a calming effect. Remember that all mammals have a pulse. Feeling our own internal rhythm not only anchors us within ourselves but connects us to all life.*

TRIGGER: After you turn off the television (or computer) and before you move on to the next thing . . . or when you simply need a fresh perspective.

TOOL: Rub your hands vigorously together to create heat and friction in the palms of your hands. Then cup your hands over your eyes. Let your eyes and face relax under your hands. Feel the pressure of your fingers on your forehead. Feel the palms of your hands covering your eye sockets. Notice temperature—are your palms warm? Are your fingertips cooler? After several seconds (up to a minute) remove your hands, open your eyes, and imagine seeing your world with fresh eyes, as if you had just returned from a long and difficult journey.

I was lucky enough to spend most of four decades of my life with twenty–twenty vision. At forty I was *shocked* to find that I couldn't read without glasses. It started with menus in restaurants. "Can't they turn up the lights in this place?" I'd mutter. It wasn't the lights.

I bought over-the-counter readers and placed them in my purse, in the car, and in every room in the house. Over time I purchased progressive strengths: 1.0, 1.5, and finally 2.0.

One day, I read about Chinese *qigong* eye exercises designed to improve vision. I started doing them because they felt soothing to my eye muscles. Although I still seemed to need my readers, what came of this exercise for me was that it reenergized me with a fresh perspective. I found myself both relaxed and seeing differently.

At the time, I had recently seen the movie *Cast Away* with Tom Hanks. In it, the main character survives an airplane crash but is cast away on a deserted island for over four years. In that time, he survives by sleeping in a cave, catching rainwater for water, and eating raw fish. I walked away from that movie with a renewed appreciation for everything from shoes and grocery stores to soft beds and even dentists (imagine trying to pull out your own tooth!).

So when I covered my eyes, I imagined myself "cast away." And when I uncovered my eyes, I saw my life in crystal clarity—a marvel of modern miracles and conveniences. Try using whatever unpleasant settings might resonate for you—being in prison, returning from the dead, being trapped underground, returning from a different time dimension—and then come back to your current life. Wow! Things never looked so good.

PURPOSE: *When we give our eyes and minds a healthy rest, we anchor ourselves in the moment. Visualizing the world afresh, we create perspective and stimulate gratitude.*

FANCY FEET

TRIGGER: **During television commercial breaks.** Suggestion: Mute the commercials so you can focus without distraction.

TOOL: **Put your bare foot in your lap and lace your fingers of the opposite hand between your toes** (your little finger will be next to your pinky, pointer next to the big toe). Spread your toes out wide and use your hand to wiggle your feet back and forth. Let yourself be aware of the stretch. Feel the pressure between your toes. Be aware of the many bones in your feet and how they support your entire weight.

I was born with long, skinny feet that turned inward . . . you know, pigeon-toed. My mother spent years (so she tells me) massaging my feet so that they would fall in the proper alignment. As a toddler, I wore special shoes. Fortunately, I did outgrow this condition and I was able to feel normal . . . sort of.

The thing is, I still had long, skinny feet. And as I grew, they got longer and skinnier (at last count, size 11AAAA). In my youth, we had to go to a specialty store an hour away just to find shoes that would fit me. I felt like I had narrow clown feet, like a ruler. If I asked for my size in traditional shoe stores, they actually laughed at me.

As an adult, I've been able to buy shoes online. I learned to wear thick socks when I couldn't find shoes narrow enough. I managed. As for my feet, I tolerated them with a certain begrudgingness.

Then, two interesting things happened. My second husband, upon first seeing my naked feet, thought they were the most beautiful feet in the world. (Awwwwww—how could I not love the guy?). He told me that they were gracile. (I actually had to look that word up in the dictionary to discover that it means "gracefully slender.") So I began to see my feet a little differently.

The second thing that happened was that on a yoga retreat, the leader had us do this exercise of threading our fingers through our toes. I had never done this before. It felt relaxing to stretch my toes in a way that they had never experienced.

I found myself cradling my foot. And as I did so, I felt an unexpected tenderness for my feet that have carried me through my world for nearly half a century. Wonderful feet! Useful feet! Dependable feet! Thank you, feet!

PURPOSE: *The meditative quality of this tool activates the calming effects of the parasympathetic nervous system. Giving our feet a unique kind of stretch builds gratitude for a part of our bodies that support us every day of our lives. Gratitude is one of the key ingredients of inner peace.*

DIAL IT DOWN

TRIGGER: **When your heart is racing.**

TOOL: **Begin counting backward from one hundred by threes (one hundred, ninety-seven, ninety-four, ninety-one . . .) very slowly. Imagine dialing down your heart rate on each number. Use your hand to turn counterclockwise turning down an imaginary dial. Exhale deeply on each turn of the "dial."**

My daughter Victoria was very energetic when she was ten years old (and hasn't changed as a teenager). She's naturally gregarious, extroverted, and passionate. We were once dining at a pizzeria— a giant cavernous room with high ceilings and loud music. Being hopped up on chocolate milk and the giggles, she began to get rather loud and rambunctious.

Out of the blue, my twelve-year-old son said to her, "I need you to dial it down, Victoria," and then he turned his hand in a counterclockwise circle. I laughed out loud, wondering where he had ever learned such a thing. When I asked, he said that he didn't know, but surprisingly, Victoria did quiet down.

So I began to experiment to see if one could "dial down" not only high energy levels but also distressing moods and even heart rate. Personally I am no stranger to the effects of adrenaline coursing through the body, be it from a temper flare-up (I am a redhead, after all) or performance anxiety.

For me, even though I have been singing in public for virtually my entire life, I still suffer from stage fright. And in fact, even if my performance is in the evening, I will wake up that morning with a racing heart. Now when I wake up, I spend portions of the day in preparation by dialing it down.

Putting my attention on counting backward by threes has the added advantage of engaging my mind in a concentrated effort, thus taking the attention momentarily off of my impending performance.

Then I have a much better chance to enjoy myself and to, uh . . . break a leg!

PURPOSE: *When we use our minds to lower our heart rates, we automatically begin to calm the body and induce a more peaceful state.*

Anxiety—often signaled by a racing heart—can be thought of as intense energy that has become temporarily misdirected. Using this thought, breathing and imagery tools help shift the energy.

Think Again

Shortcuts to Quiet Your Mind

If you've ever tried a formal "sitting" meditation or even just tried to quiet your mind before you sleep, you'll know that your mind will inadvertently stray, jumping around from topic to topic. The Buddhists call this "monkey mind."

I had a new appreciation for this term after Dan and I visited one of several Monkey Forests on our trip to Bali, Indonesia. I was very excited to enter the sanctuary that was known for its friendly but mischievous long-tailed macaques. I adore all kinds of animals (growing up, I was the kid who wanted to be a veterinarian), but truly, this adventure was unlike anything I had ever imagined. It reminded me a bit of a vacation I took with my family when I was young, driving into a wild animal safari park where monkeys were free to jump on your windshield (picture two little girls in a giant station wagon squealing with delight). But this time, I wasn't in a car, and there was no windshield to protect me.

Right at the Balinese stone gate, we watched a cute little monkey trying to steal bananas from a fruit vendor. As we ventured down the trail into the junglelike forest, the brazen monkeys jumped right on our shoulders and clung to our heads. They grabbed at Dan's sunglasses and pulled on my earrings. Unnerving as this was, it was also exhilarating. We made our way to a bench right in the heart of the monkey sanctuary where, for over an hour, we sat watching the monkeys leap on unsuspecting tourists, pull food out of backpacks, and generally whip up a lot of mischief . . . just like our minds do.

If I had to pick the most significant stumbling block to inner peace—we're talking *major* interference—it would have to be the mind. The mind has the potential to be a wonderful life-enhancing tool, but it can also be a hindrance. The mind is known to make tough situations tougher . . . the mind can exacerbate every stress, turning any molehill into a mountain. And the mind is so sneaky that most of the time we don't even realize that its meddlesomeness is responsible for our difficulties.

Here's an example that I often share in workshops to illustrate how different thoughts in the mind lead to different feelings. The facts: John is thirty minutes late, stuck in traffic, and he hasn't called home. Susan is at home waiting. How she feels will depend on what she thinks.

Susan's thought #1: *Oh good. I'm glad that John is running late so I can finish watching my TV show. I really needed this extra time to myself.*

Susan's feeling from thought #1: Relief, gratitude

Susan's thought #2: *Oh my gosh. Why is John so late and why hasn't he called? Maybe he was in a car accident. Oh no! What should I do?*

Susan's feeling from thought #2: Fear, upset

Susan's thought #3: *Where the hell is John? It's suspicious that he hasn't called. Is he still at the office? Maybe he's having an affair with someone. I could just kill him!*

Susan's feeling from thought #3: Anger, betrayal

Do you see how mischievous the monkey mind is? Generally speaking, the mind rarely ever stops monkeying around. The good news is that we don't have to pay attention to all of those thoughts. If Susan had simply observed her thoughts, watching them come and go, but not getting caught up in them, she might have just taken action and called John to see what was really going on.

The following section of Shortcuts is designed to loosen the mind's grip on our reality. They help us keep the mind as our best friend, not our worst enemy. One key strategy to this perceptional shift is to see the mind for what it is—a tool for organizing thoughts and filtering facts. In Eastern traditions, those with this witnessing ability are said to be "awake." Research in neuroplasticity supports the idea that through self-reflection, we can actually form new neural pathways in ways that are beneficial to our mental health. Learning to observe the mind at work, doing its thing, is a vital skill to cultivating inner peace.

TIME TRAVEL

TRIGGER: When feeling overwhelmed or frightened by present circumstances.

TOOL: Close your eyes, take a deep breath, and ask yourself, "Will this matter in a year? In five years? In fifty years?" With each jump in time, picture yourself in the future looking back at the situation behind you.

My husband and I like to have picnics in a nearby historic graveyard—during the day, of course. It's not that we're macabre or death-obsessed. The truth is that we don't have a public park nearby, and the graveyard is a quiet, secluded place. But there is another benefit and that is sharing the peacefulness with those who have left behind the worries of life. *Relax,* they seem to say. *Appreciate the little joys of living.*

We live in a death-averse culture, but many ancient wisdoms say that death is our greatest teacher. Making friends with the grim reaper can lead to some remarkable insights. Dan and I walk around the grassy knolls, looking at the intricately carved stones. There are Burt and Ida, who died fifteen years apart from each other, in 1891 and 1876, respectively. There's Martha, who buried three children during her sixty-six years of living. There's Samuel, who died at the tender age of eight years old, in 1850. There are dozens of babies, siblings, and spouses who lived their lives, felt their losses, agonized over their dramas, experienced their joys and now, their lives are over.

Do they care anymore about the recent blizzard, the harvest, or planting the crops? Are they troubled by political arguments at the town hall, tiffs with their relatives, financial woes? In five years will it matter to me where my daughter went to college? She'll be out of college and on to the next unknown. Will I recall this month's cable bill? Will a minor misunderstanding with my sister matter?

Take a mental trip through time to give yourself a chance to realize that most situations resolve themselves one way or another. Every situation is over eventually. So today, is any situation really worth giving away your inner peace? Take what actions you can, knowing that one day soon it will all be in the past.

PURPOSE: *Developing a larger awareness of our circumstances opens us to moving forward with less stress. Imagining ourselves in the future gives us a necessary perspective on our situations. With a little distance, we can breathe deep, let go, relax, and let life unfold as it will.*

TAKE DICTATION

TRIGGER: When your thoughts are driving you crazy.

TOOL: Write for one to three minutes, taking dictation from your mind.

PART 1: Follow your stream of consciousness by writing down every thought. For example: *This is a stupid exercise. I don't know what to write. Oh, what are we having for dinner? I can't remember who's picking up Bobby from Little League. I'm going crazy—how will I ever get everything done?*

PART 2: Go back and reread your stream of consciousness and reflect on each thought from an observer's perspective. For example: "Wow, she sounds really nervous. Look how she gets herself in a frenzy."

When I graduated from college in 1985, I didn't have a job. Still, I picked a favorite city in which to live and I plopped myself in an apartment. Looking back, I can hardly believe my chutzpah. I actually moved to New York City with no job, no connections, and no prospects. (Some might call it insanity!)

Every day I scoured the want ads and dropped into temp agencies, where I was instructed to take typing tests and asked whether or not I could take dictation and write shorthand. This was the era before computers were a standard in every office in America, but still, even then such secretarial skills felt antiquated.

I had an unusually fast typing speed and so I was quickly sent off to various temp jobs, one of which ended up to be a more permanent position (well, temporarily). But I'll never forget how humorous the thought of taking dictation was to a snippy liberal-arts college graduate.

Fortunately, the concept is eminently useful as a tool for observing yourself, for taking dictation *from your own mind*. It's a wonderful freedom to be able to watch your mind and be slightly detached from it. *Oh, there goes my crazy, nervous mind, worrying about what my boss will think* or *Yep, those are my anxious thoughts that keep me from wanting to go to social events* or *There are those same old thought patterns about not having enough money.*

Because we don't have to believe every thought we have, we can watch our thoughts, label them, laugh at them, and gently release them. We can start to see them for what they are—just thoughts and not necessarily *reality*.

PURPOSE: *Getting our thoughts out of our heads and onto paper so we can analyze them with some objectivity reduces stress by loosening attachment to negative thinking. We begin to notice patterns and thought loops that don't necessarily serve us. As we do this, we develop the capacity to observe our minds, its patterns, and our habitual responses, and we prepare the ground for new responses to emerge.*

TRIGGER: When you're waiting in a line or have an unexpected wait (for a download, in a doctor's office, for a prescription, on a phone call).

TOOL: Ask out loud, "What do I need to remember?" Keep asking yourself this question until you start to get substantial answers like "I need to remember what really matters in life," "I need to remember that I love my husband and I'm committed to us," "I need to remember how lucky I am to have healthy children," "I need to remember how grateful I am for my life," "I need to remember that on my deathbed, none of these worries will matter," or "I need to remember that this too shall pass." When the answer comes to you, feel the emotions behind the remembrances and let them flood your body.

I have had the privilege of making presentations about grief for over twenty years. I say privilege because whenever I talk to an audience about grief, whether it's a room full of seasoned mental-health professionals or a small group of community members in a library, the topic touches people in a deeply personal way. We *all* know about loss; it is the most universal of experiences. And so, people react in heartfelt ways.

If I'm doing a formal presentation of two hours or longer, I use

PowerPoint and DVD clips to make the talk more visually interesting. For many years, I have returned time and again to a clip from the Disney classic, *The Lion King*. In this animated film, the lion cub Simba is present during the death of his father, Mufasa. Innocent Simba believes that he somehow was responsible for his father's death, and overcome by guilt, he runs away to the jungle where he lives for many years. There is a scene in which the spirit of Mufasa appears in the sky and talks to his frightened son. He tells Simba that he has forgotten who he is and that he must take his place in the circle of life. Mufasa says, "Remember who you are. You are my son and the one true king."

So it is for many of us—not that we get to be king, mind you—but we forget who we are in the circle of life. We forget what matters. (Hint: It's not stuff or status.) We get bogged down in the piles of mail, bills, to-do lists, obligations, expectations, and disappointments. We forget to notice the beauty of life, the daily blessings available to us in each and every breath.

As grievers know better than anyone, life is brief and life is precious. This Shortcut helps us stop, cut to the chase, and remember that life is a *gift*.

PURPOSE: *When we cultivate positive emotions, we reduce our stress. Redirecting our thoughts to life's big priorities helps snap us out of patterns of stressful thinking. When we remember what truly matters to us, we foster feelings of gratitude and inner peace.*

GLAD GAME

TRIGGER: Whenever you find yourself in a difficult or uncomfortable situation.

TOOL: Think of three things that you're glad about even in this unpleasant moment. They can be things that you're glad are not happening or things that you're glad are happening. Feel the gladness, let yourself smile. The motto for this tool is "Things could always be worse."

One summer afternoon, my mother and I were walking in Washington, D.C., near the museums of the Smithsonian. A gusty wind swept down the street followed by storm clouds blotting out the sun. We knew that rain was imminent, but we still had several blocks to our car . . . if we could only make it before the heavens opened.

Lightning lit the sky; thunder boomed. The air whipped so suddenly that it took my baseball cap right off my head. And then the downpour began. People around us gasped and darted to the nearest museum entrance. The rain beat down furiously and relentlessly, drenching us within seconds. We ran with the crowd and crushed into the foyer of a museum filled with soggy pedestrians.

My mother sighed and grumbled. People around us, many of whom were trying to calm crying children, also sighed and grumbled. I closed my eyes, took a deep breath, and said, "I think now would be a good time to play the Glad Game."

"What's that?" asked my mom.

"It's a game started by Pollyanna. I play it all the time with the kids." Pollyanna is a beloved fictional character in a book by the same name written in 1913 by Eleanor H. Porter. Pollyanna has an optimistic knack of finding things to be glad about even when the situation is dire. Ever since reading the book, I've used it with my kids whenever we find ourselves in troublesome situations.

"I'll go first," I suggested. "I'm glad that I'm with my mom." (We don't live near each other so it's always a treat to spend time together.) "I'm glad that I don't have a screaming infant with me." (Being surrounded by screaming infants can be rough, yes, but actually being responsible for the screaming infant is another level of misery.) "And lastly, I'm not vomiting." (My kids and I have a joke that I *always* use this one in the Glad Game.)

My mother joined in happily. "I'm glad that we had this museum to dash into. I'm glad that our car isn't too far away. I'm glad to be with my daughter." (And we hugged.) Yes, we were sopping wet and mashed into a small space like human sardines, but we found a way to divert our attention from the unpleasantness and redirect our energy toward gratitude.

PURPOSE: *When we focus on the positive even when something negative is happening, we learn to redirect our thoughts and stop wallowing in misery. Gratitude and perspective are direct routes to inner peace.*

TRIGGER: When feeling stressed or when you simply need a break in your day.

TOOL: Close your eyes and mentally imagine yourself on your most relaxing vacation. Perhaps it was last year on your annual fishing trip. Perhaps it was that once-in-a-life-time trip to Europe. Perhaps it was camping out in a national park or lying on a tropical beach. Choose a memory associated with this deeply peaceful and happy time, and allow yourself to reconnect with the feeling. Recall as many details as you can: What was the weather? What were you wearing? Were there tastes and smells? What were you seeing and hearing? Breathe the memory into your body and savor it.

There were some fabulous advertisement jingles and tag lines that I remember vividly from my coming-of-age years in the seventies. One that stands out quite vividly in my mind was a 1980 commercial in which the famous line "Calgon, take me away" was coined.

The Calgon fantasy, aimed at overwhelmed women, showed a woman stressed out by messy kids, an overbearing boss, or a barking dog. Then, as she uttered the words, "Calgon, take me away," she was instantly transported to a bubble bath where she lost herself in luxury.

There's something replenishing about getting away, leaving the to-do lists behind, and escaping from ordinary living. Taking a brief "mental vacation" helps you reconnect with that feeling of relaxation. Whether you imagine your return to the same beloved campsite or recall a major international adventure, sink into a moment reveling in your trip (whether it be one you anticipate, one that you reminisce about, or one that you fantasize about).

Take a "Calgon moment" as you close your eyes and transport yourself to a place of suspended routines. Often we are at our most relaxed and most present when we're on a vacation, even if it's just visiting relatives in a neighboring state.

Connect with a joyful memory (or fantasy), and live it in as much detail as possible: Let the vision take you away.

PURPOSE: *When we redirect our thoughts to memories of a calm place and a happy time, we are reminded of our potential for inner peace. Focusing our minds on pleasant memories boosts our spirits.*

❧

TRIGGER: When you hear yourself using negative words and phrases.

TOOL: When you begin describing yourself, a situation, or another person negatively, backtrack and replace the negative words with more positive words. For example, if you hear yourself saying, "It's just been insane at work—a total nightmare," say, "Scratch that—work has been really challenging for me lately." As you become more aware of your negative words, you will begin to replace them even before you say them. Common negative words to watch out for are *terrible, horrible, awful, miserable, catastrophic, disastrous, hate, crazy, insane, overwhelmed, dreadful, nightmare,* and the like. Cancel the negative expression out and then substitute words like *challenging, full* (for *busy*), *abundant, opportunities to grow, rich learning experiences, teachable moments, fascinating,* and *curious.*

When I was growing up in Texas, I had a real bona fide southern granny. She had been raised in Paris, Texas, and was something of a beauty queen. She held the distinction of having been crowned Miss Paris in the local pageant. Her small-town glamour was matched by her other southern qualities: She could cook grits, southern fried steak, fried okra, black-eyed peas, and chess pie; she could play the piano by ear, her signature song being "Harvest Moon," and she was bossy.

I remember playing with my sister at her house, where we would often argue about a doll or a toy. My granny would bellow, "Stop fussing!" Usually we continued to "fuss" until she threatened to slap our knuckles with a wooden spoon. (I think she would have done it too, so we always immediately halted our antics.)

She had a collection of porcelain cats that created hours of fun—and controversy—for me and my dear little sister.

"That's my cat!" she would shout.

"You're so *stupid.* You're such an *idiot.* Give it back *now*," I'd say in a not-so-charming tone.

Granny would come over on her high horse and chastise us: "That kind of language is so ugly—pretty girls like you are just ugly, ugly, ugly when you use such vile words."

I'm not sure that her efforts succeeded in ridding us of our ugly language but I do think of her as I hear myself and others talk about our lives in routine conversations. Listen to the sorts of words that most people use: "Our vacation was a total disaster." "My job is crazy and overwhelming." "Losing his job has been a nightmare for the family." "She's a real bitch to work for."

Harsh and unkind words can feel heavy, weighty, negative, and dark. They create a feeling of despair and disrespect just in their utterance. Even when you feel that your situation is dire, you can use this Shortcut to redirect your thoughts toward gratitude, optimism, and/or acceptance. Drop negative words from your personal dictionary. When you notice one—backtrack and substitute it with a lighter word.

PURPOSE: *When we root out negative words from our conversations, we make room for positive energy, optimism, and hope. Even as the circumstances remain unchanged in our lives, cleaning up our language will create an energetic shift that causes us to feel better. Words do matter!*

TRIGGER: Before checking your e-mails and/or before clicking the Send button when you send e-mails.

TOOL: Take a deep breath and repeat a positive phrase (or word) while exhaling deeply. Some suggested phrases to use are "I trust"; "Calming my mind, I relax"; "Everything is as it should be"; "Peace"; "Joy"; "*Om*"; "I am filled with peace"; "Let it be"; "This too shall pass"; "I accept what is"; or even "The sun'll come out tomorrow." For added focus, close your eyes and say the words out loud, repeating your chosen mantra several times.

TIP: Write these phrases or words on note cards and keep a small collection in your desk. Post a new card/mantra each week.

My favorite musical when I was a little girl was *Annie*. I don't know why, but I was captivated by that redheaded, doggedly optimistic orphan Annie. And the songs were just so singable! I used to listen to the album over and over again. I was overwhelmed with excitement when, as a teenager, my family went to New York City for Thanksgiving and we got to see *Annie* on Broadway!

Since then, I've even had the thrill of participating in a community theater production of the musical. It's fair to say that I love

Annie! Why? I think I'm attracted to her spunky spirit. Annie was an orphan during the Great Depression. She was persecuted by the evil Miss Hannigan and eventually got scammed and kidnapped (talk about stress!). Still, she maintained an optimistic attitude, which she even used to inspire President Franklin D. Roosevelt himself.

Annie had the habit of using positive expressions, like "The sun'll come out tomorrow" and "You're never fully dressed without a smile." You could say that she *lived* by them. In fact, most of us live by certain repeated messages that loop through our conscious and unconscious minds all the time. Unfortunately, most of them are negative, such as "I'll never have enough money," "I can't do anything right," "Life is hard," and "It's a dog eat dog world out there." Sound familiar?

This Shortcut is designed to give our minds some new food for thought. Repetition conditions and shapes thought patterns. Furthermore, repeating certain words and phrases has the power to actually change our behaviors—think of the little engine whose mantra "I think I can" helped him to actually get up that steep mountain. Why not repeat and savor words that lift, inspire, and calm you? Get in the habit of using this tool throughout the day and watch yourself live into those qualities. You will create a ripple effect throughout your life that will astound you.

PURPOSE: *Repeating positive words or phrases generates positive emotions. Redirecting our thinking in this way gently directs us to a more peaceful state, creating a more tranquil energy for our day.*

Magic Glasses

TRIGGER: When feeling bogged down and unable to move forward with a task, duty, or job.

TOOL: Close your eyes and imagine yourself putting on a pair of magic glasses. These glasses allow you to see the world from someone else's perspective. For example, put on the glasses of a Broadway star . . . or the glasses of a college professor . . . or the glasses of a CEO . . . or the glasses of a saint . . . or the glasses of a truly cockeyed optimist. Try on these fabulous glasses and see the world through fresh eyes.

I am not an athlete. In fact, I'm about as far from athletic as a person can get. I was the kid who was picked last for every team in elementary school. I was the kid who tried and quit every sport that existed. I even failed at tetherball.

I have crafted an adult life that carefully avoids all exercise except for yoga, and even then, I don't like to get my heart rate above meditation level. But something happened recently that left me so demoralized that I actually bought a treadmill (though my sister warned me it would become a drying rack for my laundry).

What was the precipitating event to this rash acquisition? Well, it had to do with a visit to my seventy-year-old mother and a failed attempt to keep up with her morning walking group. Let's just say that being outdistanced by a pack of grandmas left me completely humiliated.

My treadmill gathered a lot of dust at first (but no laundry, mind you). Then, one day, feeling especially stiff in my sedentary state, I discovered the "Magic Glasses" Shortcut. Could it have been the recent winter Olympics that inspired me? Perhaps. All I know is that as if by magic, I could *see* what it might be like to get excited about exercise, to be pumped up to work out, to be psyched to reach a physical goal. I had "put on" the glasses of an Olympic athlete!

Now I rarely exercise without first putting on these glasses. I've also discovered the Patient Mother glasses and the Confident Speaker glasses. Last week I wore the I Like the Dentist glasses. Try on a pair. They work like magic.

PURPOSE: *When we imagine a different perspective, we allow ourselves the opportunity to bypass the negative, limited mind-set that gets in our way; we connect with a wiser and smarter self that knows no limits.*

TRIGGER: When you find yourself seeing life as half empty.

TOOL: After you think or make a comment that is negative, whining, complaining, or critical, follow it up with an "*And* . . . my life has many wonderful aspects too." For example, "My kids have been driving me crazy *and* I feel very fortunate that they are healthy."

When I was a young, single adult living in New York City, I had a powerful experience. The lesson learned from it will be etched in my heart for a lifetime.

I was in graduate school for social work and part of my training was an internship in a family counseling center. It was a plum assignment and I loved the work. The only inconvenience was that it involved a one-hour commute on the subway all the way to the end of the A line.

One evening I was coming home after a long day of seeing clients, and I happened to be in a car with only a handful of people. Suddenly, the door between cars slid open violently and I looked up to see three menacing-looking guys. Adrenaline coursed through my body as I prepared to be robbed or assaulted.

They moved noisily through the car whooping and hollering,

and then, one after another, they chose three targets, kicking one in the head, slamming another down to the ground, and slugging the last one in the face. I put my head down in my lap and began chanting a Hail Mary—I'm not even Catholic, but it's the first prayer that came to my mind. Then the small gang was gone, having swept through like a tornado, leaving destruction in its wake.

A woman sitting beside one of the victims began crying. I looked up at the young man across from me whose face had been pummeled—he smiled weakly, showing me a mouth full of blood and loose teeth. I quaked for several days, and even though I myself hadn't been harmed, I felt a sort of violation and shaken faith.

I went to talk with a Unitarian minister whom I heard was extremely wise and compassionate. I told him about my vicarious assault and my existential despair. He told me that yes, the world had many aspects that were vicious, cold, cruel, and heart-breaking, but the world *also* had wonder and beauty and immeasurable goodness in it. He gazed out his ground-floor window and asked me to look at the flowering cherry blossoms glinting in the sunshine. "Have you ever seen anything so beautiful?" he asked.

"The bad in the world never cancels out the good in it," he continued. He cupped his hands and held them up side by side, as if they were the balancing measures of a scale. He explained that pure wisdom was the ability to hold two directly opposing thoughts equally. Letting one hand lower below the other, he said, "Thanks to love, the bad in this world will always be outweighed by the good."

PURPOSE: *When we train our minds to see the joyful aspects of life, we tap into a deeper feeling of inner peace that keeps us floating in a world that can sometimes feel weighted by negativity.*

OUTSTANDING

TRIGGER: Whenever you are asked, "How are you?"

TOOL: When someone asks you how you are, or how you're doing, remember at least one good thing in your life and respond enthusiastically with "Outstanding," "Fantastic," "Superb," or "Awesome." It doesn't matter if these superlatives don't actually match your current mood. Focus on simple basics in your life that you can truly appreciate—like good health, a sunny day, safe children, living in a non-war-torn country. Answer the question with a descriptive stronger than "Fine" and notice other people's responses. Watch how your mood begins to shift.

I have long found the question "How are you?" utterly useless. And I've found the standard reply "Fine" equally as useless. Yet every phone conversation with a friend, colleague, stranger—even with a telemarketer—typically begins with this utterly ridiculous ritual. I imagine that teachers of English as a second language say to their students, "English speakers will ask 'How are you?' but you shouldn't actually answer the question. Simply say 'Fine' and move on with the conversation."

Thus it was a surprise when I received a call from a colleague and he responded, "Outstanding!" to my perfunctory "How are you?" Truly, I laughed out loud. I rarely ever get such an enthusiastic response, but whenever he and I converse, he is always "amazing," "fantastic," or "wonderful."

When I queried him about his unusually robust replies, he said merely, "I see every day as a gift." What a breath of fresh air! This man isn't a cancer survivor, mind you. He's an ordinary Joe with an ordinary life but he has the great vision of recognizing every day—even the rainy, cold, stressful ones—as a supreme gift.

I've since tried this answer on for size—sort of as a science experiment—to see how an over-the-top response affects other people. What I've found is that people are, as I was, struck by surprise. They notice the enthusiasm. They might reply, "Really? What drug are you on?" or "Did something happen?" to which I simply respond, "Life." And then, not only do they seem to feel a little bit inspired, but I do as well.

So I urge you to try this simple Shortcut to inner peace. Just as the physical act of smiling signals your brain that you must be happy even if you're not, the conscious act of exclaiming extreme happiness, and watching its effects on others, starts to work a little magic.

PURPOSE: *When we find small ways to be grateful, we train our minds to focus on life as a daily gift and to spread that awareness to others. Using these turbo-charged "happy" words creates an opening in our lives for more optimism and gratitude.*

All You Need Is Love

Shortcuts to Open Your Heart

We crept quietly into the tiny, sundrenched room. I made my way to a corner, sat down cross-legged, and breathed in the heavy smell of lotus-blossom incense. At least thirty people from all nationalities were sitting shoulder to shoulder, knee to knee, waiting to hear the famous Indian teacher.

I took in details of the spiritually charged space: garlands of jewel-toned flowers draped on an altar; images of gurus, masters, and gods on virtually every square inch of wall; bells, candles, offering bowls, and statues of Ganesh and Shiva. Out of the open windows you could see the waters of the holy river, the Ganga, set against the backdrop of the Himalayan foothills.

A peacefulness descended upon us. Pilgrims, seekers of enlightenment, we waited for Vanamali to appear. She came into the room singing a devotional chant. Through the sliding tonalities of Eastern music, she resonated as we swayed to her tones, mesmerized. If love could ooze, it was oozing out of this woman's pores. Everyone in the room looked drunk on peacefulness and goodwill.

Here in the holy city of Rishikesh in northern India, my best friend and I found ourselves in this holy woman's presence hoping to learn about the ancient teachings of Lord Krishna and the Vedic way of life. We expected it to be educational and interesting but instead, we found it to be transformational.

Vanamali stopped chanting and said that she would like to teach us about the most important aspect of life. We collectively leaned in, expectant, eager for this slender woman to reveal the mysteries of the universe. Her voice lowered to a whisper as she intoned, "Love." She paused, looking around from person to person, "Love is the most important energy that exists. In its purest form, it requires no gratitude . . . no reciprocation . . . no return. Love itself is its own reward."

Hmm . . . it felt radical. Growing up in America I learned about a kind of love that was more concerned with getting what I wanted, getting my needs met . . . and, by the way, what have you done for me lately?

She went on to say that when you love with an expectation of appreciation, thanks, devotion, loyalty, dependence, or praise, then you are not loving from the most pure, most sacred space. You are loving with strings attached. Wow. I was thunderstruck. Practically everyone I knew, including myself, either consciously or unconsciously loved with strings attached. Was it possible to love as selflessly as she described?

After her talk, she invited us to ask questions. People asked about suffering, about struggles, and about purpose. Somehow her answer always came back to loving from the pure place, the place of giving without needing anything in return.

After I left India, her words often came back to me. However, I didn't experience that kind of truly openhearted love until about a year later when I was attempting to comfort my sixteen-year-old daughter.

Elizabeth had been angry with me ever since I divorced her father. Two years after the fact, she still ranged from cool and distant to outright hostile. If I said, "I love you" to her, she responded with a stony silence. She wasn't particularly helpful around the house, and her general demeanor was cranky and cross. It was impossible to tease out how much was postdivorce trauma and how much was ordinary ornery teen behavior.

We often bickered, both of us behaving in childish ways. I'm ashamed to say that I rolled my eyes at her as often as she rolled her eyes at me. Rather than recognize her attitude as the hurt and tender thing that it was, I internalized her nastiness as a narcissistic injury and responded accordingly. I frequently thought, *Bitch,* as I left her room, one failed peace treaty after another.

Like most mothers, I wanted my daughter to love me. I wanted her to be happy with me, to stroke my ego, and to assure me that I was a wonderful mom. I wanted gushy cards on Mother's Day, fun lunches, laughter, and respect. Instead, I had a surly teenager who despised my very existence.

One day in the midst of this dynamic, Elizabeth hit her head on a low-lying pipe in the library. The school nurse called me to say that Elizabeth was in the infirmary and was resting before her examination by the doctor. I immediately rearranged my afternoon and drove right over to the health center.

Let's just say that Elizabeth wasn't pleased to see me. Although I had hoped that in her compromised position she might reach out to me for maternal comfort, instead she groaned, "What're you doing here? I don't want you." I felt a pang of embarrassment as the nurse who had brought me to the room coughed, turned her head, and said, "I'll just leave you two alone."

I told Elizabeth that I was going to stay until she met with the doctor and that I would just sit quietly beside her. The blackout blinds were drawn, making the room completely dark. I tried to pat her arm, but she muttered, "Don't touch me."

I sat in a chair, in the dark, beside a daughter who rejected me. I thought to myself, *This has to be the worst mothering moment that I've ever experienced.* Then, teary-eyed, I started to reminisce about when she was young and sweet, a golden girl with a sunshine smile who used to shower me with drawings of rainbows and flowers and "I love you, Mommy" hearts. How I loved that dear child. With clarity, I suddenly connected that *this* suffering adolescent was *that* dear child.

And so, just like that, as light flooded into my heart in this darkened room, I experienced the pure place that Vanamali had described: the sacred love with no need for thanks in return. As I closed my eyes and breathed deeply, I imagined streams of bright light emanating from me to Elizabeth. The love filled me to overflowing. It didn't matter whether my daughter loved me back. It didn't matter whether I received acknowledgment or confirmation. The love was coming through me, from me, for her, filling the room.

Thus my worst mothering moment instantly became my best mothering moment. I know that the energy of the room shifted because when the nurse came to get Elizabeth to take her to the examination room, she asked, "Would you like your mother to go in with you?" and Elizabeth answered, "She can come."

Love is not about eliciting a response from the other. It almost has nothing to do with the other, in the end. It has to do with you and your heart and letting it fill to overflowing with grace and gratitude. Like the story of the Grinch whose heart grew three sizes, nearly bursting out of his rib cage, my heart expanded that day. I was the one who benefitted.

Pure-hearted love leads to inner peace. These Shortcuts cultivate gratitude, loving feelings, and an open heart—qualities that help *you* feel right with the world.

TRIGGER: When hearing or seeing emergency vehicles, such as a fire truck or ambulance, and/or passing the scene of a car accident.

TOOL: When you see a trauma scene, or when you hear emergency vehicles, say, "I wish you well" or "God bless you, every one." Be aware of these people in need, people who started an ordinary day just as you did only to come face-to-face with some sort of unexpected mishap or disaster. Be aware of those who are helping them, those who are witnessing the event, and those family members and professionals affected by these activities in the hours ahead. Shower your goodwill and blessings toward them all.

For two consecutive Christmas seasons, I had the good fortune and pleasure of playing Tiny Tim's mother in *A Christmas Carol* at a local community theater. As Mrs. Bob Cratchit, I blamed Scrooge's miserly ways for the hard times that had befallen my family. So when Bob proposed a toast to Mr. Scrooge as the "founder of the feast," I huffed the line, "Why should we drink the health of such a stingy, unfeeling man?"

Why indeed? But I relent for Bob's sake, and so in the spirit of the day, we toast to his health. In this moment, Tiny Tim lifts a small glass, raises his hand high, and offers his famous toast: "God bless us, every one!" Each night, the audience predictably let out a collective, sympathetic sigh.

Tiny Tim is a good-natured, kindhearted, and generous spirit. He doesn't bemoan his crippled leg. He isn't angry at Mr. Scrooge for working his father to the bone, all for a pittance. Tiny Tim doesn't discriminate between those who "deserve" a blessing and those who don't. He just opens his little heart and blesses us all, every one.

How often are we as generous as Tiny Tim? Isn't it easy to get stuck in our routines, our agendas, and our quick-paced schedules— so much so that we close our hearts to tragedies happening all around us? Have you ever encountered a traffic jam from an accident and, even as you saw the ambulance speeding to the scene, thought, *Oh great—now I'm going to be late!* I know that I have, though I'm not proud of such self-serving sentiments. The poor person about to be placed in an ambulance was no doubt going to be even later.

The next time you encounter a speeding emergency vehicle of any kind, use it as an opportunity to stretch your heart a little wider. Use it to get out of your own myopic perspective and imagine the struggles of all the people connected with this unexpected event.

PURPOSE: *Whenever we open our hearts to those around us, we cultivate a little more inner peace in our lives. Compassion not only reduces our stress, it leads to peacefulness.*

TRIGGER: When you kill a bug.

TOOL: Say, "Peace be with you" or "Bless you" or "Safe journey," to acknowledge the death of a living creature and remember the fragility of life.

"What's the state bird of New Hampshire?"

"The *mosquito!*"

This was one of the first jokes I heard upon moving to the Granite State. And then I learned of a prestigious annual civic award known as the Mosquito Trophy given to a person whose individual efforts made a difference in the community. "Anyone who underestimates the power of One to make a difference hasn't had a single *mosquito* buzzing in their ear in the middle of the night."

I thought everyone was making much ado about nothing until my first summer in my new home. Sure enough, they were right. The mosquitoes were as thick as thieves. I thought they might lift my children off the ground, whisking them away to distant mosquito lairs. Walking outside at dusk, the mosquitoes were often so thick that my limbs looked like they were covered with dark hair.

So began a long and fruitless battle of the species: humans versus mosquitoes. We tried your basic OFF! spray as well as organic versions, citronella candles, major pesticides, magnet zappers, and good old-fashioned hand swatting. Before slumbering each night, my husband and I spent at least ten minutes scouring the walls around the bed and waging war. After one particularly bloody battle (the humans won that round), I felt a twinge of unease for leading such a massacre. And so I started chanting "*Om* peace amen" before each and every bug murder. "Nothing personal," I would add.

I liked this habit so much that when I found myself releasing any bug from this life—the occasional bee, wasp, stink bug, spider, housefly, or dreaded horsefly—I would accompany the swat with a chant of "*Om* peace amen." For years, in fact, this was my refrain for honoring their ended lives and wishing them well on their next journey, wherever that might be.

I didn't realize how ingrained this little mantra was in our household until I began to hear my children chant the same words whenever *they* killed a bug. In fact, they believed that everyone said it—like saying "Bless you" after a sneeze.

Once, when I was watching a beautiful sunrise, out of respect and reverence I muttered the words "*Om* peace amen" to which my daughter asked me, "Did you just kill a bug?" I had to laugh.

PURPOSE: *In connecting with the cycle of life and death, we honor one being's end and realize that we too are part of the same cycle. Let us seize our own lives with gusto, knowing that they are almost as brief as a bug's.*

WHO IS YOUR MOTHER?

TRIGGER: When you are in front of a cashier.

TOOL: Look at the person in front of you and for a moment internally reflect on the question *Who is your mother?* Shrink this person to a small child and imagine his relationship with his mother. Consider whether it was a happy or strained relationship. Imagine that relationship today, full of joys, struggles, expectations, and lessons in letting go. Recognize that this person, like yourself, has a history, a family, a mother. Breathe in the relationship between this stranger and his mother, and breathe out compassion to them both.

When I was about twenty-six years old, I walked into a small-town convenience store in the Catskills of New York on a Sunday morning in May to pick up some milk. As I was checking out, the older gentleman behind the counter handed me a beautiful long-stem white rose. He said, "I don't know if you are one, but happy day to you." I had absolutely no idea what he was talking about.

I went home and told my husband, who laughed and chastised, "A mother . . . it's Mother's Day today." Honestly, I had no idea (guess my own mom didn't get a Hallmark card *that* year).

Not everyone is a mother, but everyone has a mother or came

from a mother. It's kind of an amazing concept when you stop to think about it. Every single person on this earth was born from the body of a mother. Maybe it was in a hospital room, maybe it was in a back alley. Some of us knew our mothers most of our lives; perhaps some among us lost our mothers during childbirth. Maybe we were raised by a nonbiological maternal figure. But every one of us came from our mother's womb.

Furthermore, many of us have issues of one sort or another with our mothers. At some point, almost all psychotherapy explores one's relationship (or lack thereof) with one's mother. Whether we didn't get enough love or got too much smothering, it's inevitable to have some psychological dynamics around the mothering that we received.

So, consider this man or woman before you, in front of the cash register, and think for a moment about his or her mother. Imagine a relationship that might have brought great love or great confusion or great grief. Imagine times of rich complexity—tenderness between a mother and her child as well as times of disappointment and heartbreak. Let this connect you for a moment to a stranger.

PURPOSE: *When we align with the human condition, we get outside of our own little spheres, thus generating compassion. We dissolve the barriers between us and others and wake up to our interconnectedness.*

TRIGGER: When reading the newspaper or listening to the news on the television, radio, or Internet.

TOOL: As you read the newspaper (or listen to news) about things that distress or upset you, take a moment to imagine your "peace place" (a memory of a purely peaceful moment). Take a deep, full breath, and then, slowly and fully, breathe out love and light to the world. On your next in-breath, breathe in the suffering in the world. Finally, breathe out love and light and say, "I wish you peace."

I have a confession to make: I don't read the newspaper. Nor do I listen to news on the radio or television. I know, I know—it seems crazy. Almost everyone I know is a news junkie to one degree or another. People like to know what's going on. They like to follow politics, sports, world events, and local happenings.

But I don't. I never have. At first, when I was younger, the reason I didn't keep up with the news was because I was too busy—that was my excuse. Then it was because I had young children and, again, not enough time—another excuse. But the truth is that when I did occasionally read the paper (my husband at the time was an avid reader and subscribed to three papers), I got very upset. It seemed that every story I read was a tragedy, and I ended up feeling hopeless and helpless.

I once went on a weeklong urban retreat through a local Buddhist center and the first recommendation was to go off all news for the week—a detox from the negative energy of news. For me, that was easy. Done.

That's not to say that I don't ever know what's going on. I get pop-ups on my Yahoo! homepage. I scan newspapers when I'm getting a latte at Starbucks. I see the headlines in grocery store aisles. If something major happens, I hear about it. And even then, I still find myself starting to slip into the feeling of helplessness or, worse, apathy and disinterest.

So I started implementing this tool to help myself cope with painful news: international earthquakes and devastation, local murders and fatal car accidents, plummeting economy and sluggish housing markets. When I hear or read about these calamities, I stop for a moment. I breathe out love and light. Then I breathe in the pain, and finally, I breathe out love and light again. And then I invoke healing with the statement, "I wish you peace."

Why breathe in someone's pain or misfortune, you might ask? Isn't that just going to make things even harder to bear? This is a technique known as *tonglen*, most popularly discussed by the renowned Buddhist nun, Pema Chödrön. She advises that practicing *tonglen* (exchanging yourself for another, taking in their distress and sharing your peace) has the effect of opening your compassion and stimulating your ability to provide healing.

PURPOSE: *This Shortcut helps us cut through the habit of detachment and provides a way to connect to the human condition, thus increasing empathy and hope.*

❧

TRIGGER: When paying bills.

TOOL: While you pay bills, whether you're writing a check or paying online, give thanks for each service you receive. Try saying, for example: "I thank you, electric company, for the electricity that I depend on"; "I thank you, phone company, for my cell phone, which makes my life so much easier"; or "As I pay my rent/mortgage, I give thanks for this place that I call home." Really experience feelings of gratitude and let them sink in. Every bill that you pay provides you with some goods or service that you have cause to rejoice in.

One bitterly cold winter in New England, we had a massive ice storm. It was one of the largest ice storms in decades. Everything was coated in a glistening, twinkling, *deadly* sheen. Giant tree limbs snapped liked twigs under the heavy hug. Power lines were down in dozens of communities. Schools and businesses closed in a state of emergency while power-generator sales soared.

My family, like all the others, pulled out every candle and flashlight that we could find. We hunkered down for a night of firelight and giggly adventure. But how quickly the fun turned to inconvenience: no lights anywhere, no computer, no screens of any kind, no hot water, no phone, no stove, no flushing toilet, no *heat*. How quickly inconvenience turned to danger.

Being a modern, on-the-grid suburbanite, I'd never gone more than a few hours without electricity. Like any self-respecting, spoiled twenty-first-century person, I took it for granted that the flip of a switch produced *light*. I never even stopped to consider that my hot shower came from a water heater powered by electricity. I always turned the knob on my oven to find instant heat.

But that day and into the night, being without electricity brought a whole new level of awareness—and gratitude—into my life. I could just kiss that Thomas Edison for his invention of the lightbulb—and I wanted it back!

Fortunately, modern living was restored to us in less than twenty-four hours. Others were not so lucky. Church basements became makeshift shelters. Homes with power became impromptu refugee camps. Some families went a full seven days without electricity and heat even though power companies were working round the clock to restore utilities. What a winter!

For quite a few weeks after that, many of us from the icy communities got down on our knees with gratitude as we paid our electric bills. For once, we happily wrote the check that powered our lights, our heat, our cell phone chargers, our computer screens, our hair dryers, and our hot water. We even appreciatively paid the bills for our credit cards, our student loans, our car tune-ups. Suddenly modern conveniences never looked so good.

PURPOSE: *When we notice the simple, taken-for-granted luxuries in our lives, we cultivate gratitude for our modern bounty. A regular gratitude practice calms our stress response and increases our feelings of inner peace.*

TRIGGER: While drying off after a shower or bath.

TOOL: Imagine yourself as a baby and remember how perfect you were at birth. Now look at each aspect of your body, starting from your toes and moving up to the top of your head. Note and thank several miraculous parts of your body for doing their job so efficiently. Say, "I thank you, toes, for enabling me to walk"; "I thank you, knee, for making my leg work"; or "I thank you, kidney, for cleansing my system." Focus your attention on each part of your body that you thank. Make peace with your body, even with all its seeming imperfections.

I have a confession to make. It's not something I'm proud of, but there was a time when I *hated* my body. When I was a teenager and a young adult—even though I was tall and willowy—I believed that I was fat and unattractive. Years and years of journaling about my weight, my diet, my weight goals, my despised attributes (flabby thighs, protruding belly) chronicle a journey through body distortion. What a waste of adolescent energy.

I know from flipping through virtually any women's magazine and seeing titles like "Whittle Down Your Waist" or "Eliminate the Bulges" or by watching the diet industry's ever-expanding profits and never-ending gimmicks that many grown women still hate their bodies. What a waste of adult energy.

The tide irrevocably turned for me at the age of twenty-nine when I finally got pregnant with my first child (after trying obsessively for two long years). There I was with a seed growing within me all on its own. I didn't have to do anything except eat, sleep, and take prenatal vitamins. My body knew exactly what to do—what a miracle! I was the earth mother, the goddess of life, the vessel of all creation. I walked the streets aglow with the knowledge that my body could bear life.

And it did, three times. After that, even though I gained forty pounds with each pregnancy, and even though I had stretch marks to prove it, I had a limitless respect and admiration for my amazingly resourceful body. I vowed to hold only love and adoration for this temple of life.

Furthermore, as I held each precious infant, so recently released from the womb of growth and creation, I marveled at the perfect little ears, precious little fingers, amazing little digestive tracts. Could anything be more amazing to a new mother? And these masterful little miniature bodies grew! With food and warmth and rest, they naturally got bigger and stronger and more coordinated—a preprogrammed journey to thrive and survive.

I just couldn't get over it. Their amazing bodies. My amazing body. Everyone's amazing bodies. In all shapes and sizes of amazingness. And what an efficient design—cuts heal, broken bones mend, cells fight infections. It seems downright irreverent to worry about the size of one's thighs when we have opposable thumbs.

But what about the bodies that break down, you ask? What about the creaking, aging, wrinkled wear-and-tear models? I say, Love the whole process. Love that they're doing exactly what they're supposed to do. Even with sick bodies, there is something healthy to focus on—eyesight, hearing, the body's ability to fight for a cure.

So I invite you to make peace with your body—the one and only body that you get in this lifetime. Yes, one day it will wear out completely. But until then, think about how many daily miracles occur just in the process of waking up each morning. Think about how many times your heart will continue to beat without any conscious work on your part, enabling you to live this brief, precious life. Have compassion and love for this body shell that houses your soul and recognize how hard it works on your behalf.

PURPOSE: *Let us fall in love with our own bodies and accept their miraculous properties. When we wage war with our bodies, we lose. When we love our bodies, we win. Accepting our beloved bodies (in their totality) with gratitude leads to a deep peacefulness.*

Rags to Riches

TRIGGER: Whenever you think, *I don't have enough money.*

TOOL: Close your eyes and say, "I have abundance in my life." As you say this, remember the things you currently cherish: your spouse, children, family, friends, health. Think too of this rich and plentiful planet that sustains life: golden sunshine, soft rains, stunning flowers, plants and animals in a delicately balanced ecosystem, food producing fields and jungles. Keep broadening your perspective until you see that in so many ways, you are very, very rich.

I admit that I'm the kind of person who not only enjoys but actually *requires* a lot of silence and solitude. As a writer and a therapist with a home office, I don't spend a lot of time in social settings. I don't have water-cooler encounters, company Christmas parties, or big staff meetings. Sometimes it can feel a little lonely, yes, but by and large, I've created an independent, intimate work life that suits me.

I also come from a long line of obsessive-compulsive neatniks on both my mother's and father's sides of the family. Following my legacy, I tend to prefer my environment orderly, uncluttered, and tidy.

And so, you might imagine that in the summer of 2008, when

I moved into a three-bedroom home with my beloved fiancé and our *five* combined children, a little bit of chaos ensued for me. I discovered that although I had more or less adapted to my own biological children's mess patterns, I didn't have the same genetically induced tolerance to the messiness of two stepchildren. Nor did they have much tolerance for my higher-than-average tidiness expectations.

Ah . . . what a summer. Here I was poised to begin a new blended family life—a life that I fervently desired—and yet the growing pains of mashing two family systems into one felt overwhelming at best and intolerable at worst. On top of the clutter, the noise, the high energy, and the emotional strains, we actually added three new kittens to the mix. What was I thinking?

At the end of that summer of extreme transition, I was on a boat with my dear friend Martha, riding out to a retreat island that we visit every year. I had never felt so happy to get away, and I wondered vaguely if I had the stamina to return to my life. As we rode on the open sea, I felt exhausted, beleaguered, self-pitying. *Ridiculous,* I thought, *to be so whiny and pathetic after I have finally gotten to create a home with my soul mate.*

I sat quietly, wrapped up in my own drama, when an acquaintance, who happened to be on the boat, came over and struck up a conversation with us. She chatted about this and that as I looked disinterestedly out to sea. Martha engaged in the conversation and then chimed in on my behalf, "And Ashley recently moved in with her fiancé and is now raising *five* children."

"Oh really," responded the tall silver-haired woman. She looked me straight in the eye and said slowly and deliberately, "Then you are a very rich woman indeed."

I knew instantly that she meant I had a full and abundant living situation . . . though I did think for a brief moment that she was implying that I needed to *be* a very rich woman to pay for their endless expenses.

For the rest of my time on retreat, her words echoed in my ears: *You are a very rich woman.* Indeed. Yes. Just like that, a shift began to happen within my heart. Though my circumstances had not changed in the slightest, I began to feel the difference between thinking one way (five children—ugh, overwhelming chaos) and another (five children—abundance, blessing, wealth).

And from that moment on, I began to experience the expression "change the way you look at things and the things you look at change." I began to notice richness everywhere.

PURPOSE: *When we train our awareness to focus on wealth, our experience of it grows. When we have the temptation to focus on lack, dissatisfaction, or scarcity, this tool helps us shift to a perception of fullness and abundance. Having such an open and full heart leads inevitably to inner peace.*

TRIGGER: When you feel emotionally shut down or lonely. This tool is also useful when you are grieving, separated from a loved one, or are overwhelmed with sadness.

TOOL: Close your eyes, breathe deeply, place your hand over your heart, and imagine a person or a pet whom you love dearly. This beloved could be either alive or dead, either part of your present or part of your past. Think of a time when you were together and you felt deep love rise up within you. Remember the details—was it on a vacation, in your home, in the woods, during a meal? Recall the feeling of love and notice how it feels in your body. Hold that emotion and let it radiate within you.

One of my favorite books is E. B. White's classic tale *Charlotte's Web*. My mother read it aloud to me and I read it aloud to my children. You probably know the story of the extraordinary friendship between Charlotte the spider and Wilbur the pig. When Charlotte learns that Wilbur is destined for the slaughterhouse, she spins the words *Some pig* into her web to help draw attention to him (*Some spider*, if you ask me!).

Additional "webcasts" attract media attention to Wilbur and ensure a trip to the state fair. Wilbur becomes too famous and too beloved to end up as breakfast bacon, and thus Charlotte succeeds in her quest to save his life. She does this because she loves him, and of course that's what you do for a dear friend. When Wilbur cannot return the favor by saving her life, he can at least protect her egg sack and welcome Charlotte's many babies.

When I remember the people in my life who have touched my heart, changed and fortified me, my heart begins to open like a blooming rose. Feelings that you give attention to are the ones that grow. So for today, rather than feed anger or sorrow, feed the flower of love within you. Whether your experience of love was yesterday or many years ago, the love lives within you still.

PURPOSE: *When the heart remains closed, it gets brittle and bitter. A heart needs to be expanded, used, filled. We can use this tool to hold our attention on that which is good and loving. And with practice, we can change emotional patterns in our lives, learning how to open to love. Loss, pain, fear, and sadness are real emotions that sometimes threaten to lock one's heart away; remember that love transcends them all.*

BLOOMING

TRIGGER: When feeling afraid or shut down.

TOOL: Ball your hand into a fist and put it over your heart. Breathe in deeply—as you exhale slowly and fully, turn your fist around so that your pinkie is near your heart and your thumb is facing outward. Slowly open your hand like a blooming flower and say, "I open my heart to love."

It was a chilly spring night in New Hampshire. The smell of incense wafted through the open windows of an eighteenth-century church. About forty of us were gathered for a *kirtan*—the ancient Indian devotional practice of call-and-response accompanied by piano, harmonium, or drum. I felt self-conscious sitting in the wooden pews of our Puritan ancestors who surely would have been surprised to hear Sanskrit chanting in their humble dwelling.

Many people swayed and raised their hands in response to the rhythmic sounds. I sat listening, more observer than participant. I wasn't sure why I felt so still, so reserved. The sounds and smells were no longer foreign to me, as I had spent quite a bit of time learning about Eastern spiritual practices. And yet, I simply felt closed . . . somehow shut off.

Almost as if sensing my condition, the leader stopped his chanting and announced that he was going to conduct a visualization exercise with us. He continued to play his keyboard quietly and then he asked us to close our eyes and imagine our hearts. He asked us to focus on our heartbeats and see if we could conjure up an image of our hearts. I immediately got an image of a rosebud.

He then asked us to hold the image and be aware of any obstacles around our hearts. It was all a little unclear to me until he asked us to release the obstacles and free ourselves. In that moment, it was as if threads that had been holding the bud in tightly vanished. As I "watched" this image, the bud began to bloom. My heart "blossomed" and I felt myself expand with love.

I have continued to use this tool to keep my heart open and blooming. Honestly, it takes a lot of energy to keep a heart closed down. Having an open heart simply feels better. I notice that when my heart is in full bloom, everything in my life flows more smoothly, from interactions with my husband to exchanges with tollbooth attendants.

PURPOSE: *When we develop the practice of keeping a softened heart, we find that our stress diminishes and serenity becomes our more frequent companion. Inner peace thrives when our hearts are receptive, accepting, and giving.*

TRIGGER: When you feel your heart shutting down from fear, judgment, resentment, or blame.

TOOL: Put your arms behind your back and clasp your hands. Inhale deeply as you lift your heart up, squeeze your shoulder blades together, and turn your eyes up to the sky. As you exhale slowly, say, "I love and I am loved."

In the early 1990s I had a very interesting volunteer position: running bereavement support groups through a hospital in Greenwich Village. The type of loss and the manner of loss were the same for each of the young men in the groups—their partners had died of AIDS.

Over the course of several years I ran many groups, and while each griever was, of course, individual, there were universal themes in their struggles. There was the shame of their partner having died of AIDS. There was the realistic concern (and often reality) that they would contract the disease. There was the shared experience of multiple losses, as many of these men knew dozens of people in their community who had been felled by the disease.

To my surprise, however, there was an extremely common

shared experience among these men that I hadn't expected, that of having been ostracized by their biological families. This surprising reality came up over and over again as I watched grown men cry when they described being rejected by their own mothers.

I was a young mother at the time, and I found it impossible to imagine shunning any of my children simply because they had grown up to be a person whom I hadn't expected. I began telling my toddlers that they could do anything, be anyone, love anyone, and I would always accept them. My precocious son asked, "Even if I was a crook?" "Yes," I assured him, "even if you were a crook."

I am often surprised by how conditional our alleged unconditional love is. We tell our children that we love them, but what we often mean is, "I love you as long as you choose the schools I want you to go to, the person I want you to marry, the religion I think you should practice, the job I think is in your best interest." Or "I love you deeply as long as you don't disappoint me by becoming a drug addict, alcoholic, shoplifter, sex offender, liar, or cheat."

True unconditional love is as open and as inclusive as the universe itself. It spreads past galaxies and galaxies to the great beyond. Most of us have trouble with it because we can so easily get hurt, feel afraid, and cast blame. And when we feel those things, we shut down like a snapping turtle on its prey. We get so wrapped up in ourselves that we fall into the self-pity pit.

It never feels good to shut down our hearts in bitterness or

Wake Up, Little Honey, Wake Up!

Shortcuts to Connect with Spirit

When I was twenty-five, I had my very own existential crisis. It felt dramatic. At the time, I worked in public relations in New York City; my job was to promote an allergy medication. But in truth, I spent my days typing, photocopying, filing, and pushing a lot of paper around my desk. My work, and by extension my *life*, felt utterly unimportant and useless.

I remember a particular walk through the crowded streets of Manhattan on a warm spring afternoon in which I reflected on the seeming meaninglessness of life. " 'What's it all about, Alfie?' " I hummed. Everywhere I looked were people involved in repetitive and mundane tasks: shopping for groceries, running clothes to the dry cleaners, picking up prescriptions at the drugstore, popping letters into mailboxes, eating in restaurants meal after meal after meal. Where was the meaning in living on the surface of life, where everything felt so super-ficial and flat?

But there, in the heart of the Upper West Side, feeling stuck in the horizontality of our pointless world, I realized that there must be some depth to this cold plane of human existence. There had to be something more, something intangible and ineffable that brought a rich *vertical* dimension to our lives, something above and below the surface, which touched the soul and transported the spirit. And I began to think of the transcendent aspects of my life, such as music, poetry, rich emotions, love, meditation, and prayer.

Yes, it was this vertical dimension that I wanted to connect with, revel in. I decided, right then and there, that I needed to take steps to become either a minister or a psychotherapist. It might have been a more interesting story if I had decided to give up everything and wander through India in search of enlightenment as the Buddha did, but for me, psychotherapy was my path.

Within a few months, I was enrolled in graduate school with the hopes of helping people explore their emotions, resolve their painful issues, and live a life more authentically vertical. And for the next couple of decades, this is exactly what I did. During this time, I saw a clear separation between that which was horizontal (dull, boring, superficial) and that which was vertical (spiritual, emotional, meaningful).

Then, one quiet afternoon, I read *The Miracle of Mind-fulness* by the Zen master Thich Nhat Hanh and my two-dimensional world expanded. Even if you haven't read this book, you might have heard of his most famous example of mindfulness: washing the dishes. He suggests that when you wash the dishes, you simply wash the dishes! Don't think about what you did at work or what you're going to do in the evening. Don't think about the television show that you're about to turn on. Don't even talk to your spouse. Just wash the dishes: Feel the water on your hands, feel the temperature, feel the smooth plates.

Mindfulness, of course, is the complete and exact opposite of multitasking. Multitasking, which Western society adores, urges us to perform multiple tasks simultaneously, whereas mindfulness, which Eastern society relishes, suggests that we focus on one task at a time. Personally, I've never been particularly skilled at multitasking (it makes me nervous), but I had never considered that washing dishes (a horizontal activity for me) could be an opportunity for spiritual awareness (a vertical activity).

I slowly came to realize that *every* horizontal activity could be infused with a kind of vertical awareness. And the flat two-dimensional image of life that I had held in my mind's eye, where the horizontal intersected the vertical, suddenly blew open. The lines of my conceptual world became three dimensional, if you will, expanding and growing. Every point in my world became a place for both the horizontal and vertical aspects of living.

I no longer divide life into the horizontal and the vertical.

No activity exists on its own accord. Just as we can feel dull and distracted while taking a nature walk or listening to a symphony or sitting in front of a guru, we can have spiritual awareness while cleaning a toilet or chopping carrots. The activity itself is in many ways irrelevant—all that matters is whether we're allowing our inner spirit to be present. In other words, we don't require a Himalayan mountaintop because the mountain is actually within us.

I finally recognized that the big dichotomy in life wasn't between the horizontal and the vertical; it was between being "asleep" and being "awake." To be asleep was to live on automatic pilot, unconsciously careening through mind-numbing day after day, foot to the pedal but driving around in circles. To be awake was to live with intentionality and choice, deliberate conscious experience and reflection, interconnectedness and gratitude: to live with awareness.

Therefore, inner peace wasn't to be found by avoiding the mundane tasks of daily living in favor of poetry, love, and spirituality. Inner peace was to be found by waking up to the beauty and stillness of our everyday lives in perfectly ordinary moments, each of which has the potential to be extraordinary.

The Shortcuts in this section are not about changing our daily activities. They're simply about helping us wake up to the pervasive energy that infuses the planet with beauty, goodness, and love. This energy is called by many names, but in my personal experience, I know it to be both beyond us and within us.

Once we begin to awaken to a larger perspective, all frames

of awareness begin to expand. We start to shift into the acceptance of life rather than resistance to it, trusting that there is an order even when we cannot see it. True inner peace, in the end, can be accessed by one simple word: *Yes*—saying yes to life in all of its manifestations (including sickness, aging, change, rainy days, and even death). Once we practice getting in touch with accepting the flow of life, we find that it's possible to feel as centered and peaceful in a hospital waiting room as it is on a massage table.

Sound crazy? Awakening to Spirit cultivates an inner alignment with the universe, which gives us glimpses of grace and peace in an otherwise chaotic world. We may notice the surface waves, sometimes smooth and sometimes choppy, but they don't really matter when we are suspended in the calm, deep waters.

TRIGGER: Before beginning a meal.

TOOL: Open your hands, palms up, on either side of your plate in a gesture of receptivity and gratitude. Or you may prefer to put your hands together in the traditional prayer, or Namaste, pose, and bow to your food in a gesture of thanks. Let yourself feel the emotion of gratitude and allow it to flood your body like a nutrient.

When I was growing up, the only time we said grace was at my grandparents' house. It was a rather formal affair and only my grandfather was allowed to say the actual blessing. We held hands, closed our eyes, and he intoned a Christian prayer by rote. I must say that the experience didn't do much for me. It didn't make me feel especially grateful or even connected to a higher power.

Still, when my children were young, I decided that we should say a kind of blessing at the dinner table. I created a three-sentence ditty that I thought would be easy to remember (which it was). We said it diligently before each dinner: "Dear God, thank you for our many blessings. Thank you for our food. And God bless those less fortunate than us."

Sadly, this ritual didn't really make any of us feel especially grateful or connected to a higher power either. My three children often spent the holding-hands part slapping each other. But the situation really got out of hand when they started saying the words as fast as humanly possible, sometimes with mouths already full of food.

I abandoned mealtime grace. It had lost its meaning and was becoming a comedy at the dining table. Then one day, I was reading an article about early Native Americans and how their custom upon killing an animal was to thank it and bless it for its gifts. The Native Americans were all about gratitude—they appreciated the bounty from the earth, the abundance from nature. They were connected to the earth's cycles, never forgetting about their mutual dependence on the earth and the animal kingdom.

Thus inspired, I brought "grace" back into my life. And not just at dinner but at each and every meal—even a snack. I simply bow to the food and remind myself that I would literally *die* but for this food. Food keeps me alive and thus I am grateful to it. And since being diagnosed with hypoglycemia and recognizing my need for food every few hours lest I crash and burn, I am *really grateful* to food for keeping me afloat.

And so grace has reappeared at our dinner table. We hold hands and sing a rousing rendition of "The World Is Good to Me" sung to the tune of "The Lord Is Good to Me." This camp-song style of hearty singing has its more comical moments, but it feels joyful and authentic. And at the end, I bow to my food with gratitude.

PURPOSE: *When we consciously express gratitude for food's part in keeping us nourished and alive, we increase our level of awareness and redirect our thoughts from daily stresses to appreciation for what we have. Gratitude is strongly linked to inner peace.*

MYKU

TRIGGER: When feeling preoccupied with trivial things, when your mind feels busy and hectic, when you feel the need to "stop and smell the roses."

TOOL: The haiku is a classic form of Japanese poetry. In English, it is typically written as a three-line poem with the first line consisting of five syllables, the second of seven syllables, and the last of five syllables. A *myku* is my simpler version of a haiku, a three-line poem with no syllabic rules. Write a haiku or myku, focusing on a detail of the environment surrounding you right now. Try focusing in on something that you hadn't noticed before.

Examples:

> *dust gathers*
> *on my desk*
> *blue sky*

> *finger smudges on the screen*
> *shadows glide across*
> *the floor, dancing*

One of my favorite places on this planet is a jumble of rock islands ten miles off the coast of New Hampshire known as the Isles of Shoals. Star Island, a pedestrian-only summer retreat center draws me to its shores year after year. One year, I traveled there with a group of poets and songwriters to hone our crafts.

The first afternoon's assignment was exploring the island, looking for minute details, and translating our discoveries into poetry. I had a lot on my mind that summer. I was in the middle of a divorce, which was dominating my every waking thought. In fact, I imagined that I'd be writing divorce poetry over the weekend! But trying to be the good student, I attended to the task of examining the island habitat and weaving my discoveries into words.

I chose the haiku because it is so simple and so focused. After a while, to free myself, I began to write three-line poems with no meter, which I named a "myku."

What I discovered on that sunny August day was that I got relief from my own mind. All my concerns about division of property, child custody arrangements, parenting plans, 401(k)s, alimony, life insurance, health coverage—not to mention grieving lost dreams and worrying about my children's reactions—evaporated. My stressful ruminations were stilled for the moment as I turned my attention to the delicate Queen Anne's lace and the seagull cries and the salty air.

I learned that by shifting my attention, not only could I experience a respite from my troubles, but next to the beauty of creation, my concerns actually shrank in size. We all spend a lot of time in any given day paying attention to negative stuff: our aches and pains, the bills, the pressures at work, unwelcome conflicts, complaints, and worries. Allow yourself a moment to write a myku about the details around you, and let the experience reunite you with your miraculous world.

PURPOSE: *When we focus our attention momentarily away from whatever it is that preoccupies our minds, we gain perspective on our worries in comparison to the magic of the world around us.*

HOT AIR

TRIGGER: When you're worried.

TOOL: Imagine yourself up in a hot-air balloon looking down on yourself. See the whole picture of your life in the context of the world. Take a deep breath. As you breathe out slowly, relax your shoulders and say to yourself, "The world is large and I am only a small piece in the puzzle of it."

When my children were young, we went on a ski trip to Utah. I've never been much of a skier but I was looking forward to seeing the natural beauty of Utah. While there, we decided to take advantage of an exciting opportunity: a hot-air-balloon ride.

Somehow I imagined this to be a simple afternoon outing. Instead it turned out to be a life-changing experience.

My first husband and I, our three young children (ages nine, seven, and five), and about eight other assorted tourists climbed into a large basket, which then proceeded to lift into the air powered by nothing more than a whole lot of hot air.

My first reaction was panic. My thoughts became slightly obsessive: *Is this safe? What if the hot air stops and we plummet to our deaths? What if someone jumps overboard?* As my panic rose, I imagined huddling at the bottom of the basket in a fetal position.

And then I heard the angelic voice of my nine-year-old daughter peering over the side of the basket: "Cool. Look over there. Look how big the world is." She offered me the gift of perspective and the challenge of getting out of the prison of my own mind.

And so I looked over the edge and felt the bracing air on my face. I pointed at the objects below and marveled at the mountains. We all became so absorbed by the majesty of this beautiful earth seen from above that my worries no longer seemed significant.

Now when I find myself preoccupied by the useless agitation of worry, I picture myself up above, mesmerized by a beautiful view, seeing my life as a speck in a vast world.

PURPOSE: *When we gain some perspective on our situations, it can be a tonic for our weary, worried minds. Remembering that the world does not revolve around us gives us the freedom to relax and experience inner peace.*

TRIGGER: Whenever you talk about the weather or are reacting to the current weather conditions.

TOOL: When you catch yourself complaining about the weather, *stop*. Instead of joining in with the grousing, simply say, "Really? I love this weather." Usually that produces a shock effect. If saying this feels like too much of an inauthentic stretch for you, then simply state a fact, such as "Yes, it has been raining for five days now" or "It snowed twelve inches yesterday." If you cannot be positive, at least try to be as neutral as possible when describing the weather. Remember that all kinds of weather are necessary to keep this earth healthy. So remain neutral and notice how almost everywhere you go, people complain about the weather.

I have lived in some pretty extreme climates. Growing up in Texas, it was routine to have summer days with temperatures topping one hundred degrees. And yet I never remember complaining about the weather. As kids, we just played and enjoyed whatever weather the earth provided. It wasn't until I became an adult, living in the Northeast, that I noticed the popular sport of "weather bashing."

One of my personal favorites during New Hampshire winters

is "I can't stand the snow." I want to say, "Really? Then why are you living in New England?" Don't get me wrong . . . I have done more than my fair share of complaining about the cold in New England. I have extremely poor circulation and spend much of the year with freezing fingers and toes. I've also moaned about the rain that once lasted all of June. I've grumbled about shoveling snow and complained about the wind and single-digit temperatures.

However, one day in the bleak of midwinter a few years ago, a shift occurred for me. I was in a restaurant having lunch with a friend when I saw a man walk by in a T-shirt proclaiming in neon green letters NEVER LET THE WEATHER DETERMINE YOUR MOOD.

Wow. This idea had never occurred to me. Why indeed let the weather determine my mood? Weather can't be controlled—it can barely be predicted. It changes all the time and cannot be influenced by any force on earth. Why let something so unpredictable be the basis for my daily mood?

Since then, I've practiced a more neutral response to weather. It's true that I don't especially love bitter temperatures. And no, I don't love extreme heat either. In fact, my ideal comfort zone lies in the very small window between 65 and 80 degrees (which means I'm usually not all that comfortable). But I am something of a weather champion these days. I get a kick out of watching people's faces when I talk about loving the rain. I watch myself start the car in subfreezing temperatures, teeth chattering, thrilling to the bracing air.

And guess what? No weather pattern lasts forever. So relax, watch it change, and keep your mood out of it.

PURPOSE: *Remember that our earth home requires all kinds of weather to keep it healthy and balanced. When we complain about the weather, we leach negative energy into our minds and bodies. Resisting something that you have no control over is futile. Making friends with what is generates positive energy which spills over into your life as inner peace.*

WHITE FLAG

TRIGGER: When you are afraid of an outcome over which you have no control (like the result of a medical test or admission to a college).

TOOL: Close your eyes, breathe in, and imagine yourself holding a pole with a white flag on the end of it. As you breathe out slowly and deeply, let your shoulders relax, imagine waving that flag to the right and the left, and say the words, "I surrender to what is happening. I surrender to what is about to happen. I surrender to this process."

I was sitting in the doctor's examination room waiting for the results of my trusted friend's sonogram. We were to find out if the tumor was operable or not. I began examining the playful wallpaper of puppies, kittens, and bunnies that surrounded us. My golden retriever nuzzled my hand and softly licked my fingers.

Hickory was almost twelve years old and had been like a second son to me. I first laid eyes on him when he was a week old, and he came home as an official family member two months later. Since that time, he has watched three children grow up around him.

Now he had within him a tumor larger than a grapefruit. Prognosis still unknown, though cancer was likely. Surgery was uncertain. And so I sat and waited for the test results. And as I sat I closed my eyes in reminiscence. I thought of the many times he had chased squirrels—always optimistic that he might actually catch one even with twelve years of failure. I thought of when he had watched over feverish children, sat patiently under my desk as I wrote, and cowered at even the most distant clap of thunder. Our dear Hickory.

I felt a lump in my throat. Then I felt the impulse to lean into the uncertainty and let go. I waved my white flag and surrendered to a fate that was unknown at the moment but almost certainly already sealed. Praying for a desired outcome seemed almost childish, not to mention futile. The facts already existed; we just had to be made aware of them. I waved a white flag of surrender and I relaxed.

The veterinarian came in and suggested that we go outside for a walk together. Tears sprang to my eyes as I could only imagine that this mode of news delivery could only mean that Hickory's life would soon be coming to an end. I breathed in more surrender and found myself settling into a place of acceptance.

As it turned out, the cancer had not metastasized. With surgery, we had a possibility of extending Hickory's life a bit longer . . . which we did, successfully. But I know that it is only a matter of time before I say good-bye to my furry friend. And so, I enjoy his every day and wave that white flag as I surrender to the natural ebb and flow of all living things. As I accept this reality, I feel at peace.

PURPOSE: *When we willingly surrender to the greater forces of the Universe, forces that we cannot control, we feel a deep peacefulness that settles into our bones and aligns us with the natural order of all things.*

TRIGGER: Whenever you're feeling frustrated, tense, or unbalanced.

TOOL: Close your eyes and sit comfortably. Say the syllables *SA TA NA MA* over and over again. While doing this, touch your fingers to your thumb on both hands simultaneously, like this:

> Thumb to pointer finger—say *SA*
> Thumb to middle finger—say *TA*
> Thumb to ring finger—say *NA*
> Thumb to pinkie—say *MA*

> Repeat the sequence first out loud, then in a whisper, then silently in your head: *SA TA NA MA*

Not long ago, I was at my desk facing a writing deadline, a client due in a half hour, a pile of bills that needed to be sent out, a list of phone calls that needed to be returned, and a general mile-long to-do list. It was one of those days when it felt like I would never get everything done (and as it turned out, I couldn't).

In the midst of this snowballing energy, the phone rang. I didn't pick it up. However, letting my curiosity get the better of me, I listened to the message and found that my dentist's office wanted to confirm my cleaning for next week. Normally, this would be a helpful call since I'm all for reminders. *But* the office assistant wanted me to call her back to confirm that I had received the message. *"What?"* I fumed. (Think camel's back. Think straw.) "I have five kids and a husband with a million doctor and dentist appointments to coordinate and they *never* ask me to call *them* back! I don't have time for this."

Nevertheless, I picked up the phone and hurriedly dialed the number, all the while running a tape of very negative mind chatter through my head. And without any inner peace whatsoever, I rapidly barked out the words, "Ashley Bush. Monday at ten thirty. I'll be there." And then I hung up the phone even as the poor receptionist was just getting out the words "How can I assist you?"

Oh dear. Not very nice. My energy collapsed in on itself even as my heart started racing. I immediately felt embarrassed, off track, anxious. What to do? I remembered the *SA TA NA MA* practice that my yoga teacher guaranteed would balance my energies and restore equilibrium. At the time, I hadn't the faintest idea what the words even meant but I didn't care. I sat in my chair and danced my fingers against my thumbs, repeating first quickly and then more slowly *SA TA NA MA*, over and over again.

After saying the syllables both out loud and silently for about three minutes, I did start to feel better. My heartbeat slowed down. I began to forgive myself for my snippiness and mentally apologized to the receptionist who was only doing her job. And

I gave thanks that no other doctors' offices required a return phone call.

PURPOSE: *These Sanskrit syllables mean "birth," "life," "destruction," and "regeneration." When recited, they promote focus, clarity, and stress reduction. Saying them repeatedly taps us into the cycle of all living things. Furthermore, using this tool slows us down enough to find our center and there, we can dwell in peace.*

BLESS YOU

TRIGGER: When you find yourself having resentful, judgmental, envious, or jealous thoughts.

TOOL: Simply breathe a deep breath, and as you slowly and fully exhale, say to the recipient of your negativity, "Bless you" (as if they had sneezed). Wish them happiness and joy and genuinely mean it.

When I was a teenager, I read teenybopper magazines with zeal. I subscribed to several and looked forward to reading about the latest fads, fashions, celebrities, and tips. But I can still vividly remember an article that shocked me by its nastiness.

The article's headline was something along the lines of "She's Beautiful. She's Talented. She's Rich. We Hate Her." Wow. It starts early, the culture of women hating other women who seem to have more or have it better. Even as a teen, I was struck by how catty and spiteful the tone between women could be. The same is no doubt true between men and women and men and men as well, but our society especially showcases—even promotes—this horrible negativity between women.

What is the source of this ill will? Perhaps it goes back to our caveman ancestors—the survival of the fittest. With a limited supply of resources, another person's good fortune might mean our demise. The fit survived and the less fortunate perished.

But haven't we moved past that? Good fortune isn't finite. We live in a society of abundance and plenty. One person's happiness doesn't mean that there's less to go around. Their well-being can inspire and scatter joy for us all.

Allowing the green-eyed monster to inhabit our minds, drains our resources . . . like a subtle poison eroding our inner peace. Feelings of ill will boomerang back at us. Feeling joy at another's joy, however, liberates our spirits.

Even if we feel the impulse to hate, we have the opportunity to notice it and to release it like a balloon. When we don't feed our negative thinking it begins to evaporate and we can turn our attention to our capacity for happiness. Then we are available to scatter "Bless you" around like candy in a parade.

PURPOSE: *Wishing another joy softens the edges of our hearts and relieves the tensions and resentments that create stress. Spreading good energy is sure to return to us tenfold.*

TUNED IN

I was in seventh grade in Dallas, Texas, when I experienced my first yoga class. It was an introductory six-week class as part of our mandatory gym curriculum. We learned some simple stretches that were fun and easy. However, what I remember most was that we chanted the *om* sound both at the beginning and at the end of class.

It was hard for a group of seventh-graders to sit cross-legged and chant the *om* sound without giggling—okay, so in fact we all did giggle. And yet something resonated within me. I've carried the practice of this simple exhalation of sound on breath with me ever since, even beyond yoga class.

In the ancient yogic tradition, *om* (sounded out as *aum*) is the sound of creation, or the sound of the universe. Chanting "*Om*" allegedly links you to the rhythm of all life itself—the rising and setting of the sun, the ebb and flow of the tides, the lunar cycle, the changing of the seasons, the beating of our hearts.

I find that a simple hum of any kind acts as a kind of tuning fork, activating a vibrational energy literally within the body that tunes you to the pulsating vibrations around the earth. It just feels good, so hum away.

PURPOSE: *When we redirect our thoughts to the world outside ourselves, we feel the connection to something bigger. Our voices have the power to reduce tension in our bodies, tune our vibrational frequencies, and soothe our souls.*

LET YOUR FINGERS DO THE WALKING

TRIGGER: Whenever you feel stuck and need a break for inspiration or when you feel disconnected or discouraged.

TOOL: Use the finger labyrinth and allow yourself a moment of silence to take the journey. Use your finger or the end of a pen to trace the path. Begin at the center bottom and slowly follow the path to the inner center and back again. Try to keep your attention focused directly on the point where your pen or finger meets the paper. If you wish, you can start the journey with an intention or a question that you would like help with. *Go slowly*—this is not a race.

Until the first time I walked one, I had never experienced a true labyrinth. I was with my daughter at a retreat center and I expected this complex garden path to be like a New England autumn corn maze, a puzzle in which you could be lost for hours. Instead, I discovered that there was only one direct way in and out. This experience was not for entertainment; it was meant to be meditative.

My thirteen-year-old was not interested in a hypnotic stroll and urged me to walk a little faster so that we could get to the center. "I think the point is the journey, not the destination," I said. She wasn't overly impressed, but I remember thinking that the experience had potential.

The second time I walked a labyrinth I was on a retreat at Star Island, a stark getaway off the coast of New Hampshire. This time, alone, I was able to take my time. The experience blew me away. Every step I took seemed to be a metaphor for life: Focus on your step and don't worry about the end point; stay on the course and stop occasionally to look up and smell the roses (or in this case, the sea air); trust the process even when you feel lost. Once I got to the center of the labyrinth, I discovered a veritable shrine of stones, sea glass, bird bones, trinkets, pottery shards, and other simple treasures. Witnessing these offerings made me feel connected to those who had walked the path before me.

Since then, I have walked other labyrinths—some small and nearly lost in overgrown weeds, others large and well maintained. Each walk instills a sense of curious wonder. So you can imagine that when I discovered the *finger* labyrinth, I jumped at the experience.

Sure enough, taking a few moments to pause and enter into the twists and turns and back trackings of a labyrinth allows the mind to release for a little while. I've also been amazed how certain phrases and words pop into my head along the journey, almost like a mystical message sent to guide or comfort me. I invite you to see for yourself!

PURPOSE: *This exercise helps us stay grounded in the moment, escaping briefly from our mental madness. In stilling our thoughts, we refresh ourselves so that we can begin anew.*

This pattern appears in the nave of Chartres Cathedral in France. Constructed in the thirteenth century, it is the most popular of all labyrinth designs.

JOY TO THE WORLD

TRIGGER: When you blow-dry your hair.

TOOL: Take a moment to aim the hair dryer toward a window, out to the world, and scatter some joy. Say, "I spread joy out to all beings on the planet." Think of grievers, people struggling with loss, illness, addiction, fear, anxiety, depression, people in hospitals, prisons, people getting divorced, people getting married, people having babies, people struggling with infertility, victims of natural disasters—and let yourself experience goodwill as you blow it out to the world. Share your compassion for the entire human condition.

The first time I ever saw a Tibetan prayer wheel in person was, surprisingly, at the state fair of Texas. There I was, walking with my dad amid the fried-butter booth and the Fletcher corn-dog stand, minding my own business. We had just left the animal area where we had watched a mother pig nursing her twelve babies. We turned left into a hall of stalls where everything was for sale, from handcrafted jewelry to cowboy hats to the latest kitchen gadgets to handblown glass trinkets.

And there in the corner, like a mirage, was a stall of all things exotic. The incense beckoned me, and trancelike, I followed. The stall was covered in colorful Indian fabrics. Statues of the Buddha and Hindu deities crowded around Nepalese trinkets. I felt I was being transported in time and space to an Eastern bazaar.

In the center of a table was a large vase filled with Tibetan prayer wheels. I had seen pictures of them before. Each had a copper, brass, or silver gem-encrusted cylinder on the end of a stick, reminding me of magic wands. Inside each cylinder was a handprinted scroll with the words *Om mane padme hum*, translated as "wisdom is within your own consciousness."

The merchant lifted one saying in a strong accent, "You hold the stick and swing this part around. The prayer inside is released to the universe to bless all sentient beings." He smiled broadly.

The act of scattering blessings out into the world to touch people's lives revives our connection with the larger world and the Spirit that dwells within and among us.

PURPOSE: *When we spread positive and loving energy out into the world, it makes us feel better inside. In opening our hearts and creating momentum for compassion and goodwill, we come out of our own small worlds and broaden our connection to something more.*

Deep Peace

She sat in the chair across from me and dabbed at her eyes with a tissue. I felt her weighty sadness and noted the strands of gray framing her face. She gazed out my office window and, with a sigh, said, "I'm missing my life. It's all going by so quickly, and I can't seem to stop long enough to feel any of it."

Gloria had just sent her firstborn, her beloved son, off to college. "When I hugged him good-bye," she continued, "I had this memory flash of dropping him off at his first day of kindergarten. Where did thirteen years go?"

Gloria could have been singing the lyrics of "Sunrise, Sunset" from the classic musical *Fiddler on the Roof.* With my own oldest daughter a year away from college, I too could have joined in the refrain, "swiftly flow the days, seedlings turn overnight to sunflowers, blossoming even as we gaze."

Gloria spoke quickly, "It's like I've been caught up in a giant, rolling snowball for years and years. My husband and I work; we raise the kids; we run errands—the snowball keeps getting bigger. We work more; the kids get busier; we run more errands. Do I ever stop for a second to even notice my life?" She choked back tears. "I feel like I've been living in basic survival mode, always rushing around, and I *know* there must be a better way. My daughter's already ten and I don't want to miss the rest of her childhood. Life is so short—didn't I just see that with my mother?"

Gloria had originally come to see me after her mother's death six months earlier, from a long and complicated illness. In fact, Gloria had chosen to be her mother's caretaker, interacting closely with hospice and participating actively in her mother's dying process. These major losses—that of losing her mother and of sending her son to college—were causing Gloria to wake up to her life.

Sometimes we need life to shake us. Typically death; the threat of death or of loss in the form of a divorce, a layoff, a serious illness; or an empty nest serves as the ultimate alarm clock. An entirely new perspective can emerge as a result of these life experiences.

I am reminded of dear old Ebenezer Scrooge, who unexpectedly and dramatically faced a vision of his empty life's end. In response, begging for a second chance, he resolved to live anew. In the final scene of the story, Scrooge's eyes and heart open to the joys of every precious moment. I believe that the reason this story captivates generation after generation is because, unconsciously, we all long for such a transformation, knowing that we too need a kick to appreciate life so vibrantly, so intensely, and so happily.

But why wait for three ghosts to come in the night to illuminate us? Why wait for a heartbreaking loss to ring the bell? Why not wake up to our life today, right now?

Gloria couldn't make up for lost time, but she could start to live in the present with more intentionality, more mindfulness, more peacefulness. She knew that making huge changes in her lifestyle wasn't realistic, but she was especially open to sliding in tools that required no extra time.

The first Shortcut that I taught her was "Take Five," to do while she was in the bathroom. She needed to learn how to breathe, how to pause throughout her day, and how to be present in a perfectly ordinary moment.

Gradually she began to incorporate more Shortcuts: "Freeze Frame" as she drank her morning coffee, "Big Sky" as she commuted to work, "Play It Again, Sam" when she did chores at night and on the weekends, and "Rest in Peace" before she fell asleep.

She also started practicing a three-minute contemplation exercise ("ABC" Connection) in the morning and the evening, which she found calming. In fact, she convinced her husband to practice this with her before they went to bed.

Over time, Gloria's resistance gave way to acceptance. Her rushing gave way to awareness. Ultimately, she confirmed that she didn't need to change her circumstances in order to feel better—in fact, she enjoyed her work, her home, and her family—she just needed to notice with gratitude, redirect her negativity, and restore herself with regular pauses.

What she also came to realize is that as a result of these

repetitive moments and these shifts of attention, her overall mind-set started to transform. In other words, she experienced peace beyond the small here and there moments. Peace became an expanded, integrated backdrop to her days and her nights. She found that she was less reactive, less on autopilot, and more open to life's richness.

Radiating Peace

I too have discovered how a lifestyle of integrating "tools to triggers" can have a substantial impact on my well-being. I continue to experience how the simplest pauses build on themselves, creating an energy that spreads into a growing appreciation of the miracle of my life.

Just as the small moments of serenity radiate outward to a broader context of calm, so the calm itself radiates outward from us. We inspire others to live more amicably, one person touching another, leading the way and inspiring the next. When we focus on waking up from the spin cycle of daily thoughts and activities, who knows where it will lead?

I welcome you to the path of peace, to finding multiple, daily opportunities for awareness, redirection, and restoration. The time is now for us to sink below the choppy waves of circumstance and relish the deep joys of being alive.

Inner peace will be ours, one Shortcut at a time.

May you come to know the inner peace that resides within you.
May you smile in sun and in rain.
May your thoughts be pure as a mountain stream.
May you feel centered and anchored in every storm.
May you be filled with gratitude for the gifts of life.
May your heart overflow with love.
May you dwell in deep peace and share it with others.

Appendices

Shortcut "Tools and Triggers" Cross-Referencing

The following pages break down the Shortcuts by type (verbal, action, imagination), by situation (mindfulness, compassion, perspective, gratitude, stress, anger, anxiety), and by the trigger.

SHORTCUTS BY TYPE

Verbal Shortcuts

If you like Shortcuts that primarily involve saying or thinking something, try these:

Daily Dose, *p. 35*
Morning Glories, *p. 37*
Catch and Release, *p. 39*
Freeze Frame, *p. 41*
Stop, Drop, and Roll, *p. 43*
Go with the Flow, *p. 46*
Big Sky, *p. 51*
Mirror, Mirror on the Wall, *p. 61*
Right Turn, *p. 75*

Remember This, *p. 153*

Glad Game, *p. 155*

Watch Your Mouth, *p. 159*

You Can Say *That* Again, *p. 162*

Half 'n' Half, *p. 166*

Outstanding, *p. 169*

God Bless Us, Every One, *p. 176*

Don't Bug Me, *p. 178*

Newspaper Clippings, *p. 182*

At Your Service, *p. 185*

Pretty Baby, *p. 188*

Rags to Riches, *p. 191*

Fair-Weather Friend, *p. 214*

Bless You, *p. 222*

Joy to the World, *p. 229*

Action Shortcuts

If you like Shortcuts that primarily involve concrete activities, try these:

Take Five, *p. 49*

Shakedown, *p. 53*

Rest in Peace, *p. 55*

My Sunshine, *p. 63*

Love Letters, *p. 66*

Rise and Fall, *p. 69*

Jack 'n' Chill, *p. 72*

Win-Win, *p. 78*

Smooth Scaling, *p. 84*

Touch Tank, *p. 94*

Lend a Hand, *p. 97*

Almond Joy, *p. 100*

Crystal Flame, *p. 105*

Double Take, *p. 107*

Stop 'n' Smell, *p. 109*

Ring My Bell, *p. 114*

A Little Night Music, *p. 116*

How Low Can You Go? *p. 124*

Dish It Out, *p. 126*

Play It Again, Sam, *p. 128*

Tap Dance, *p. 132*

Take the Pulse, *p. 136*

Eyewitness, *p. 139*

Fancy Feet, *p. 141*

Dial It Down, *p. 143*

Take Dictation, *p. 151*

Blooming, *p. 196*

Open Sesame, *p. 198*

Amazing Grace, *p. 206*

Myku, *p. 209*

Finger Food, *p. 219*

Let Your Fingers Do the Walking, *p. 226*

Imagination Shortcuts

If you like Shortcuts that primarily use visualizations, try these:

Rag Doll, *p. 81*

Cheesecloth, *p. 87*

See-Food, *p. 102*

Hair-Raising, *p. 111*

Under the Sea, *p. 130*

Be a Tree, *p. 134*

Time Travel, *p. 149*

Take Me Away, *p. 157*

Magic Glasses, *p. 164*

Who Is Your Mother? *p. 180*

Some Pig, *p. 194*

Hot Air, *p. 212*

White Flag, *p. 217*

Tuned In, *p. 224*

SHORTCUTS BY SITUATION

Shortcuts to Become More Mindful

Daily Dose, *p. 35*

Freeze Frame, *p. 41*

Almond Joy, *p. 100*

Stop 'n' Smell, *p. 109*

Hair-Raising, *p. 111*

Ring My Bell, *p. 114*

A Little Night Music, *p. 116*

Dish It Out, *p. 126*

Play It Again, Sam, *p. 128*

Tap Dance, *p. 132*

Take the Pulse, *p. 136*

Eyewitness, *p. 139*

Fancy Feet, *p. 141*

Finger Food, *p. 219*

Shortcuts to Develop Compassion

Morning Glories, *p. 37*
Win-Win, *p. 78*
Smooth Scaling, *p. 84*
God Bless Us, Every One, *p. 176*
Don't Bug Me, *p. 178*
Who Is Your Mother? *p. 180*
Newspaper Clippings, *p. 182*
Blooming, *p. 196*
Open Sesame, *p. 198*
Bless You, *p. 222*
Joy to the World, *p. 229*

Shortcuts to Increase Perspective

Big Sky, *p. 51*
Rag Doll, *p. 81*
See-Food, *p. 102*
Double Take, *p. 107*
Be a Tree, *p. 134*
Time Travel, *p. 149*
Remember This, *p. 153*
Myku, *p. 209*
Hot Air, *p. 212*
White Flag, *p. 217*
Tuned In, *p. 224*
Let Your Fingers Do the Walking, *p. 226*

Shortcuts to Enhance Gratitude

Morning Glories, *p. 37*

Freeze Frame, *p. 41*

Rest in Peace, *p. 55*

Mirror, Mirror on the Wall, *p. 61*

My Sunshine, *p. 63*

Love Letters, *p. 66*

Glad Game, *p. 155*

Watch Your Mouth, *p. 159*

You Can Say *That* Again, *p. 162*

Half 'n' Half, *p. 166*

Outstanding, *p. 169*

At Your Service, *p. 185*

Pretty Baby, *p. 188*

Rags to Riches, *p. 191*

Some Pig, *p. 194*

Amazing Grace, *p. 206*

Fair-Weather Friend, *p. 214*

Shortcuts When You Are Particularly Stressed or Overwhelmed

Catch and Release, *p. 39*

Go with the Flow, *p. 46*

Take Five, *p. 49*

Shakedown, *p. 53*

Cheesecloth, *p. 87*

Touch Tank, *p. 94*

Lend a Hand, *p. 97*

Crystal Flame, *p. 105*

How Low Can You Go? *p. 124*

Under the Sea, *p. 130*
Take the Pulse, *p. 136*
Time Travel, *p. 149*
Take Dictation, *p. 151*

Shortcuts When You Are Angry or Faced with Anger

My Sunshine, *p. 63*
Rise and Fall, *p. 69*
Jack 'n' Chill, *p. 72*
Right Turn, *p. 75*
Cheesecloth, *p. 87*
Dial It Down, *p. 143*
Take Me Away, *p. 157*
Magic Glasses, *p. 164*
Half 'n' Half, *p. 166*
Finger Food, *p. 219*

Shortcuts When You Are Anxious or Worried

Catch and Release, *p. 39*
Crystal Flame, *p. 105*
Tap Dance, *p. 132*
Dial It Down, *p. 143*
Time Travel, *p. 149*
Remember This, *p. 153*
Take Me Away, *p. 157*
Magic Glasses, *p. 164*
Myku, *p. 209*
Finger Food, *p. 219*
Tuned In, *p. 224*

SHORTCUTS ORGANIZED BY THE TRIGGER

At Home

When you wake up—Daily Dose, *p. 35*

When you brush your teeth—Morning Glories, *p. 37*

When you shower—Catch and Release, *p. 39*

When you take the first sip of coffee—Freeze Frame, *p. 41*

When you use the bathroom—Take Five, *p. 233*

When transitioning between work and home—Shakedown, *p. 53*

When you wash your hands—Go with the Flow, *p. 46*

When you're in front of a mirror—Mirror, Mirror on the Wall, *p. 61*

When you're doing chores—Play It Again, Sam, *p. 128*

When you're falling asleep—Rest in Peace, *p. 55*

When you pay your bills—At Your Service, *p. 185*

When you kill a bug—Don't Bug Me, *p. 178*

When you hear an ambulance—God Bless Us, Every One, *p. 176*

When you begin a meal—Amazing Grace, *p. 206*

When you read a newspaper—Newspaper Clippings, *p. 182*

When you notice the weather—Fair-Weather Friend, *p. 214*

When you answer the question "How are you?"—Outstanding, *p. 169*

When you blow-dry your hair—Joy to the World, *p. 229*

When you're emptying the dishwasher—Dish It Out, *p. 126*

When you have a key in your hand (to your house, office, gym locker, or car)—How Low Can You Go? *p. 124*

When you have a pen in your hand—Love Letters, *p. 66*

When you check your e-mails—You Can Say *That* Again, *p. 162*

When you're drying off after a shower or bath—Pretty Baby, *p. 188*

When you start preparing a meal—Stop 'n' Smell, *p. 109*
When you're washing your hair—Hair-Raising, *p. 111*
When you start a project—Ring My Bell, *p. 114*
When you're watching TV, during a commercial break—
    Eyewitness, *p. 139*, or Fancy Feet, *p. 141*
When you have insomnia—A Little Night Music, *p. 245*
When you have a stressful evening with kids—Rag Doll, *p. 81*
When you find yourself annoyed with a loved one—My Sunshine,
    p. 63
When you are faced with hostile energy—Right Turn, *p. 75*
When you're feeling selfish and stubborn—Win-Win, *p. 78*
When someone compliments or criticizes you—Smooth Scaling,
    p. 84
When you feel lonely—Tuned In, *p. 224*
When you are using negative language—Watch Your Mouth,
    p. 159
When you feel like you don't have enough—Rags to Riches,
    p. 191

At Work

When you take the first sip of coffee—Freeze Frame, *p. 41*
When you use the bathroom—Take Five, *p. 49*
When you wash your hands—Go with the Flow, *p. 46*
When you're in front of a mirror—Mirror, Mirror on the Wall,
    p. 61
When you kill a bug—Don't Bug Me, *p. 178*
When you hear an ambulance—God Bless Us, Every One, *p. 176*
When you begin a meal—Amazing Grace, *p. 206*
When you notice the weather—Fair-Weather Friend, *p. 214*
When you talk to a cashier—Who Is Your Mother? *p. 180*

When you answer the question "How are you?"—Outstanding,
  p. 169

When you have a key in your hand (to your house, office, gym
  locker, or car)—How Low Can You Go? *p. 124*

When you have a pen in your hand—Love Letters, *p. 66*

When you check your e-mails—You Can Say *That* Again, *p. 162*

When you start a project—Ring My Bell, *p. 114*

When you're waiting in a line—Remember This, *p. 153*

When you find yourself annoyed with a loved one—My Sunshine,
  p. 63

When you are faced with hostile energy—Right Turn, *p. 75*

When you're feeling selfish and stubborn—Win-Win, *p. 78*

When someone compliments or criticizes you—Smooth Scaling,
  p. 84

When you feel lonely—Tuned In, *p. 224*

When you are using negative language—Watch Your Mouth,
  p. 159

When you feel like you don't have enough—Rags to Riches,
  p. 191

In the Car

When you're waiting at a red light—Stop, Drop, and Roll, *p. 43*

When you get in your car/use public transportation—Big Sky,
  p. 51

When you hear an ambulance—God Bless Us, Every One, *p. 176*

When you notice the weather—Fair-Weather Friend, *p. 214*

When you have a key in your hand (to your house, office, gym
  locker, or car)—How Low Can You Go? *p. 124*

When you feel lonely—Tuned In, *p. 224*

When you are using negative language—Watch Your Mouth,
p. 159

OTHER TRIGGERS TO CONSIDER

When you turn on/off the television
When you pick up/hang up the telephone
When you take vitamins or morning medication
When you feed your pets
When you charge your cell phone
When you go to the grocery store
When you're in a shopping mall
When you wrap gifts
When you have a cocktail
When you turn on/off your computer
When you turn on/off your printer
When you get dressed in the morning
When you get undressed at night
When you make the bed
When you take off your makeup
When you tuck in your kids at bedtime
When you're shaving
When you walk up or down stairs
When you're on an escalator/in an elevator

Shortcut Contemplation: "ABC" Connection

The components of this short practice are as simple as ABC.

A—Aware: Become mindfully aware of the world around you, and notice what your senses are perceiving (sounds, smells, textures).

B—Breathe: Follow the breath as a means to calm and focus the mind.

C—Center: Focus your awareness internally, feel the energy at the core of your body, and repeat a mantra as a grounding tool.

To begin this contemplation, sit or lie down in a comfortable position. Close your eyes and give approximately one minute to awareness, one minute to breathing, and one minute to centering.

In more detail:

A—Spend one minute becoming aware. First notice your environment—pay attention to any sounds and smells around you, the temperature of the air on your skin, the texture of the chair or bed beneath you, how your body feels, and if there is tension. Notice everything around you with a calm, nonjudgmental curiosity, and if you find your mind wandering, simply label it "thinking" and return to your task of scanning your environment. This process anchors you into the present moment.

B—Spend one minute noticing your breath. Simply feel, listen to, and watch your breath. Notice the brief moment of stillness between your inhale and exhale—that space in the moment of transition. Label the exhale . . . space . . . inhale . . . space . . . exhale . . . space . . . inhale . . . space . . . and so on. Again, if the mind wanders (which it will!), label it "thinking" and then bring your attention back to the breath. Or imagine the thought as a cloud that just passes across the sky of your mind. Notice as the breath starts to draw the mind inward and prepares you for going to your center.

C—Spend one minute going to your center. Begin by imagining a column of light that runs through the body like a vertical axis—along the spine, at the core of your body—and that extends upward through the crown of the head and downward through your body. The light can range in colors and textures. Allow yourself to "merge into the center," or connect to this core column of light and energy.

Repeat a mantra, which helps to anchor the mind into this state of centeredness. The word can vary from day to day but a few suggestions are "peace," "love," "*om*," "spirit," "acceptance," "truth," "trust," "light," "flow," or any other word that speaks powerfully to you. Simply repeat the word mentally over and over, or imagine it being written repeatedly in the core of you.

To come out of this practice, reverse the ABC process: As you are **centered**, focus briefly on the **breath**, then return your attention to the **awareness** of your body in your environment. Wiggle your fingers and toes, and when you are ready, open your eyes. You are refreshed!

Shortcut Contemplation: Peace Connection

This short meditation helps you release stress and connect with your inner sanctuary. It has three structured components:

First minute—Breathe in white light (for peace) and breathe out gray smoke (for stress). Breathe deep and low in your belly. Inhale through your nose and exhale through pursed lips, as if you were blowing through a straw.

Second minute—Say, "Peace," over and over. Try to imagine the word written in front of you on a board. Experiment with visualizing different colors of the writing and different types of font.

Third minute—Imagine yourself in your "peace place." This is a place (as described on p. 14) where you have felt completely safe and happy. Try to imagine this place in as much detail as possible to truly feel yourself surrounded in that tranquil environment. Include smells, sounds, tastes, textures, and sights to complete your picture. Rest there.

To come out of the meditation, reverse the process. Say, "Peace," again several times and conclude by breathing in white light. You are refreshed!

Suggested Reading

Over the years, I have learned from many wise people, both in person and in their writings. There are, no doubt, many excellent books not included in this list. However, the following list of books and websites happened to cross my path and influence my thinking as I wrote *Shortcuts to Inner Peace.* These resources have shaped my ideas and helped elucidate my own journey to greater awareness and inner peace.

BOOKS

Alexander, R. A. *Wise Mind, Open Mind: Finding Purpose and Meaning in Times of Crisis, Loss and Change.* Oakland, CA: New Harbinger, 2008.

Baraz, J., and S. Alexander. *Awakening Joy: 10 Steps That Will Put You on the Road to Real Happiness.* New York: Bantam, 2010.

Begley, S. *Train Your Mind, Change Your Brain: How a New Science Reveals Our Extraordinary Potential to Transform Ourselves.* New York: Ballantine Books, 2007.

Bodhipaksa. *Living as a River: Finding Fearlessness in the Face of Change.* Louisville, CO: Sounds True, 2010.

Boorstein, S. *Happiness Is an Inside Job: Practicing for a Joyful Life.* New York: Ballantine Books, 2008.

Boroson, M. *One-Moment Meditation: Stillness for People on the Go.* New York: Winter Road, 2009.

Brach, T. *Radical Acceptance: Embracing Your Life with the Heart of a Buddha*. New York: Bantam Books, 2004.

Brantley, J. *Calming Your Anxious Mind: How Mindfulness and Compassion Can Free You from Anxiety, Fear, and Panic*. Oakland, CA: New Harbinger, 2003.

Byron, K. *Loving What Is: Four Questions That Can Change Your Life*. New York: Three Rivers Press, 2003.

Chodron, P. *Don't Bite the Hook: Finding Freedom from Anger, Resentment, and Other Destructive Emotions* (audio). Boston, MA: Shambhala Audio, 2007.

Das, L. S. *Awakening the Buddha Within: Tibetan Wisdom for the Western World*. New York: Broadway Books, 1998.

Germer, C. K. *The Mindful Path to Self-Compassion: Freeing Yourself from Destructive Thoughts and Emotions*. New York: Guilford Press, 2009.

Hanh, T. N. *The Miracle of Mindfulness*. Boston: Beacon Press, 1999.

Hanson, R., with R. Mendius. *Buddha's Brain: The Practical Neuroscience of Happiness, Love & Wisdom*. Oakland, CA: New Harbinger, 2009.

Kabat-Zinn, J. *Wherever You Go, There You Are: Mindful Meditation in Everyday Living*. New York: Hyperion, 2005.

Lokos, A. *Pocket Peace: Effective Practices for Enlightened Living*. New York: Penguin, 2010.

Mantell, Susie. *Your Present: A Half-Hour of Peace: A Guided Imagery Meditation for Physical and Spiritual Wellness* (audio). Chappaqua, NY: Relax™ Intuit LLC, 2000.

O'Hanlon, B. *Do One Thing Different: Ten Simple Ways to Change Your Life*. New York: Harper Paperbacks, 2000.

Prentiss, C. *Zen and the Art of Happiness*. Malibu, CA: Power Press, 2006.

Ring, P. E. *Life at First Sight: Finding the Divine in the Details*. Wilmette, IL: Baha'i Publishing, 2009.

Ringer, J. *Unlikely Teachers: Finding the Hidden Gifts in Daily Conflicts*. Portsmouth, NH: OnePoint Press, 2006.

Salzberg, S. *Lovingkindness: The Revolutionary Art of Happiness*. Boston: Shambhala, 2002.

Sapolsky, R. M. *Why Zebras Don't Get Ulcers*, 3rd ed. New York: Holt Paperbacks, 2004.

Siegel, D. J. *The Mindful Brain: Reflection and Attunement in the Cultivation of Well-Being.* New York: W. W. Norton, 2010.

Siegel, R. D. *The Mindfulness Solution: Everyday Practices for Everyday Problems.* New York: Guilford Press, 2010.

Simpkins, C. A., and A. M. Simpkins. *Zen in Ten: Easy Lessons for Spiritual Growth.* North Clarendon, VT: Charles E. Tuttle, 2003.

Stahl, B., and E. Goldstein. *A Mindfulness-Based Stress Reduction Workbook.* Oakland, CA: New Harbinger, 2010.

Talbott, S. M. *The Cortisol Connection: Why Stress Makes You Fat and Ruins Your Health—And What You Can Do About It.* Berkeley, CA: Hunter House, 2007.

Tolle, E. *The Power of Now: A Guide to Spiritual Enlightenment.* Novato, CA: New World Library, 1999.

———. *Stillness Speaks.* Novato, CA: New World Library, 2003.

Zander, B., and R. S. Zander. *The Art of Possibility.* Boston, MA: Harvard Business School Press, 2000.

WEBSITES

http://www.wisebrain.org—The authors of *Buddha's Brain* offer news and tools for happiness, love, and wisdom.

http://calmandcool.com—An online guide to being peaceful.

http://stress.about.com—An extensive website offering a wide range of resources for coping with stress.

http://www.dailyom.com—A website dedicated to daily words of wisdom to stimulate self-reflection and awareness.

http://todoinstitute.org—A website dedicated to the structured method of self-reflection called Naikan, a practice developed in Japan.

http://pemachodronfoundation.org—Articles, audio, and video on the down-to-earth teachings by the author of *When Things Fall Apart.*

Letter to the Reader:

I enjoy hearing from readers and I would especially love to hear about your experience with the Shortcuts or your own variations. Please join our Shortcut community at www.facebook.com/shortcutstoinnerpeace where I interact with people about creating more peace in our lives. For additional Inner Peace resources and links, visit www.ashleydavisbush.com.

You are also welcome to e-mail me at ashley@ashleydavisbush.com.

Wishing you much peace,
Ashley